Now and Not Yet:

Sermons of Grace and Hope

Patricia Healy Locke

Now and Not Yet: Sermons of Grace and Hope
ISBN: Softcover 978-1-949888-38-6
Copyright © 2018 by Patricia Healy Locke

All rights reserved. No part of this book may be reproduced or transmitted in any form or by any means, electronic or mechanical, including photocopying, recording, or by any information storage and retrieval system, without permission in writing from the publisher.

To order additional copies of this book, contact:

Parson's Porch Books
1-423-475-7308
www.parsonsporch.com

Parson's Porch Books is an imprint of Parson's Porch & Book Publishers in Cleveland, Tennessee, which has double focus. We focus on the needs of creative writers who need a professional publisher to get their work to market, & we also focus on the needs of others by sharing our profits with those who struggle in poverty to meet their basic needs of food, clothing, shelter and safety.

For Ashley and Ben, always

Table of Contents

Foreword 7
Let Not Your Hearts Be Troubled 9
   John 14:1-14
A Place of Holy Mystery 15
   Luke 7:11-17
Dashed Hopes to Burning Hearts 22
   Luke 24:13-49
Get in the Boat 29
   Mark 4:35-41
God Endures 35
   Luke 21:5-19
Invisible Fence 42
   Acts 11:1-18
Fearfully and Wonderfully Made 48
   Psalm 139:1-6, 13-24
Who Is the Greatest? 55
   Mark 9:30-37
Open Hearts, Willing Spirits 61
   Acts 16:9-15
Putting on Christ 67
   Romans 13:8-14
Hold Fast to Hope 73
   Hebrews 10:11-25
Salt and Light 79
   Matthew 5:13-20

What Do You Want God To Do For You? 85
    Mark 10:46-52
More Than We Know 92
    Matthew 13:31-33, 44-52
Telling Stories 97
    James 5:13-20
The First Step 103
    Mark 10:17-31
Ash Wednesday: Getting it Right in God's Eyes 109
    Matthew 6:1-6, 16-21
The Spiritual Life: Prayer 113
    Psalm 27
The Spiritual Life: Repentance 120
    Luke 13:1-9
The Spiritual Life: Extravagant Love 126
    John 12:1-11
Who is This? 133
    Matthew 21:1-11
What Kind of King? 139
    Luke 23:33-43
Easter Sunday: Only the Beginning 145
    John 20:1-18
Abundant Life for All 151
    John 10:1-10
Seeking: Epiphany Sunday 157
    Matthew 2:1-12

Foreword

I have known Patricia Locke as a writer far longer than I have known her as a pastor, but happily I was also there when God spoke into her life and called her to the life of a pastor.

For as long as I have known Pat, going back 25 years, maybe longer, she has been a person who expressed herself beautifully, with clarity and precision. She knew what she wanted to say, and she said it. She usually said it as well as it could have been said.

We were in a writers' group together, all those years ago, and when the group met we would read each other's work and offer comments about it, an important but difficult process for someone trying to make it as a writer. Commenting on what other people write, what other people sometimes love as much as their own children, is just about guaranteed to irritate and anger those other people.

But Pat never did that. As I recall, Pat's comments on what I wrote were always memorable and on target. I knew I should pay attention. So, it was in that writers' group that I learned Pat could be wise and direct and caring, traits that would serve her well later when she became a pastor.

The sermon in this collection titled "Open Hearts, Willing Spirits" describes a time in Pat's life when she experienced God making a "way open" in her life, when God called her out of her previous life and into this thing she and I call "ministry." I happened to be present when she received this call, as she notes, and I happened to walk alongside her as she responded to it, but the journey is all hers – all her courage, all her openness, all her vulnerability.

And now, it seems clear to me from reading the sermons in this collection, she has brought all of those experiences of her life, and all of her gifts as a writer, into her new life as a preacher. I think it was because she was a writer before she became a pastor that she knew how to tell a story, that she could take people with her words from point A to point B, that she was able to communicate important truths.

Not all preachers can do this, of course, as you may have noticed from listening to a few of them, but Pat can. And I have come to believe that it is a gift that cannot be taught. Pat has this gift. She still says what needs to be said, and she still says it with gentle wisdom, a disarming directness, and a writer's precision. The sermons in this collection are in many ways a distillation of her life, which means what she says is real and genuine and honest. But they're more than that. What she says is true, and because it's true, it's what you and I need to hear. It's the gospel.

-Douglas J. Brouwer,
Pastor, International Protestant Church
Zürich, Switzerland

Let Not Your Hearts Be Troubled
John 14:1-14

"Do not let your hearts be troubled. Believe in God, believe also in me. ²In my Father's house there are many dwelling places. If it were not so, would I have told you that I go to prepare a place for you? ³And if I go and prepare a place for you, I will come again and will take you to myself, so that where I am, there you may be also.

⁴And you know the way to the place where I am going." ⁵Thomas said to him, "Lord, we do not know where you are going. How can we know the way?" ⁶Jesus said to him, "I am the way, and the truth, and the life. No one comes to the Father except through me. ⁷If you know me, you will know my Father also. From now on you do know him and have seen him." ⁸Philip said to him, "Lord, show us the Father, and we will be satisfied." ⁹Jesus said to him, "Have I been with you all this time, Philip, and you still do not know me? Whoever has seen me has seen the Father. How can you say, 'Show us the Father'? ¹⁰Do you not believe that I am in the Father and the Father is in me? The words that I say to you I do not speak on my own; but the Father who dwells in me does his works. ¹¹Believe me that I am in the Father and the Father is in me; but if you do not, then believe me because of the works themselves. ¹²Very truly, I tell you, the one who believes in me will also do the works that I do and, in fact, will do greater works than these, because I am going to the Father. ¹³I will do whatever you ask in my name, so that the Father may be glorified in the Son. ¹⁴If in my name you ask me for anything, I will do it.

One year, for each of our birthdays, my mother sent my sisters and me the same birthday card. It was a cartoon of a woman wrapped in a bath towel, standing before a foggy mirror. She is reaching for her glasses next to the sink. As she squints into the mirror she says, "Mom?"

I think most of us reach the point in life when we sense we are becoming our parents. Whether this is a good thing or a bad thing, I leave up to you. I quit being flabbergasted a long time ago when my mother's words started coming out of my mouth – mostly when I was imparting some motherly "wisdom" to the kids. Sometimes I even channel my dad's horrible puns. When that happens, my son makes a great show of looking around the room and asking, "Grandpa?"

The older I get, the more often I see my mother standing in the mirror. Mom had so many delightful attributes, but God's sense of humor dictates that I should not necessarily inherit all the good traits in my parents; instead God gave me the traits that drove me the most bats as I grew up. So why am I so surprised to find that Mom and I share something else?

My parents did not spend a lot of time talking about spiritual things. They both were deeply faithful, but they led more from example than from conversation. Certainly, the topics of death and dying were held at arm's length, almost as if talking about it would cause it to happen.

Mom died in 2010 of cystic fibrosis: her lungs just slowly refused to work. She was 95 years old and still sharp as a tack. One night, before her final illness, I was visiting Mom and Dad in Arizona. My mother and I stood on their driveway, looking up at a remarkable display of stars, such as one finds only in the dry air of the dessert southwest. Somehow, heaven looks bigger out there.

Out of the blue, Mom said, "I don't want to die." Then she added, "I don't know where I'm going." Surprised, I said, "Mom, I think we both know where you're going." "I know," she replied, "but I like it *here*."

I know, Mom, I like it here, too. Now that you are gone, I finally get a small glimpse of what you meant.

Lately, I find myself thinking about all the things I want to do before I die. I don't mean some comedic bucket list. I want to know if I will have enough time to do the things I still long to do – things I think I *must* do. Can I do all of them? Some of them? Will my time on earth leave any sort of mark behind, anything at all that says, "I was here"?

I do not remember much about the rest of the conversation with my mother that night, but pray I didn't offer some stupid, cliché response. I hope I did not say something awful like, "Well, after 95 years you've had a good run, Mom." Surely, I was not that clueless – or tactless.

Of course, I know deep in my heart my mother is in the arms of the God who loves her. Still, standing on that driveway, under the stars, I never said what I might have said: "Let not your heart be troubled; believe in God, believe also in me."

In our scripture reading for today, we hear the words of comfort Jesus spoke to his disciples: "In my Father's house are many rooms; if it were not so, would I have told you that I go to prepare a place for you? And when I go and prepare a place for you, I will come again and will take you to myself, that where I am you may be also."

This scripture from John's gospel is often called Jesus' "Farewell Discourse." Jesus is preparing his disciples for his imminent death. Once more, he reminds them they are at the brink of his crucifixion, resurrection and ascension. He has just lovingly washed their feet, and now they gather around the table. In a moment, Judas will steal away and begin a dark journey of his own. Yet, despite all the times Jesus has spoken to them about it, the disciples never really understand what he is saying. Their hearts are deeply troubled, yet they do not hear his words of comfort. They only ask questions.

We do this, too. When we struggle to make sense of things, or feel overwhelmed by circumstances, we often turn to questions: why is this happening? Who is doing this? How did this happen? And, in the end, will my life have made a difference?

When Jesus says, "you know the way to the place where I am going," Thomas replies quite bluntly, "Lord, we do not even know where you are going, how can we know the way?" And when Jesus suggests that *he* is the way and that anyone who knows him will know the Father, Philip also reaches his limit and makes a request that is even more audacious – indeed, asking what no pious Jew would dare ask: "Show us what God looks like."

Jesus' answer – "Have you been with me so long and still do not know me?" – is less about his own frustration than it is an attempt to re-focus the question. Perhaps he understands that the real question is *why* – *why are you leaving us*, and *why can we not go along?* In response, Jesus offers not so much an answer as he offers himself.

Like the disciples, our hearts are troubled because the gift of mortal life does not last. What will free us? The world has a multitude of answers for us, but Jesus has only one: "believe in God, believe also in me." No matter what questions the disciples ask, Jesus begins from a place of comfort and assurance. "In my Father's house there are many dwelling places. I go to prepare a place for you, and then I will come and take you there, and you will be with me forever."

Yet these questions are important. They give voice to our deep need to understand, to comprehend, to make sense. But they are also often quite difficult, if not impossible, to answer. What should I have said to my mother? What should Jesus have said to his friends?

Part of the answer is found in what Jesus did before he departed. Jesus gives the gift of his last bit of time on earth to comfort and prepare his disciples for life without him. Remember what John's gospel records: Jesus lovingly washes their feet, shares a meal with them, and commands them to love one another. He gives the gift of himself. So maybe the question I should be asking is not, "Do I have enough time to accomplish all I desire?" The better question is, "Before I go, have I washed the feet of the poor? Shared food with those who need to be nourished in both body and soul? Truly loved others as I love myself? Have I given enough of myself – not as Jesus gives, but as he commands of us?"

If there is any way we can answer "yes" to those questions there will be no need to wonder if we will leave any mark on the world. Offering that kind of comfort and hope is the greatest legacy anyone can ever create for themselves.

Instead of answering the "why" question, Jesus answers the question of "who." He is the one who loves them and, in turn, who makes visibly clear God's love. He is the one they have known and can trust and who will do what they ask and provide them what they need.

Sometimes we want answers, even when what we really need is relationship. In our close relationships, in the kindness we leave behind, there is the best legacy of all. So many of the things we want to do are already present in the gifts we give others. So maybe my son is not so off the mark when he pretends to look for my father, because a large part of who Dad was is still here. Our departed loved ones remain present in who and what *we* are, and how the world is made better by them, even if just for a brief moment.

Messy, unanswered questions are part and parcel of our life of faith. Our brokenness means we are human. Yet, whatever our questions, whatever our doubts, whatever the unknowns, Jesus still makes himself available to us. Indeed, Jesus still offers himself to us, inviting us into a relationship that may not answer all of our questions but ultimately transcends them.

Amen.

A Place of Holy Mystery
Luke 7:11-17 - The Message

11-15 Not long after that, Jesus went to the village of Nain. His disciples were with him, along with quite a large crowd. As they approached the village gate, they met a funeral procession—a woman's only son was being carried out for burial. And the mother was a widow. When Jesus saw her, his heart broke. He said to her, "Don't cry." Then he went over and touched the coffin. The pallbearers stopped. He said, "Young man, I tell you: Get up." The dead son sat up and began talking. Jesus presented him to his mother.

16-17 They all realized they were in a place of holy mystery, that God was at work among them. They were quietly worshipful—and then noisily grateful, calling out among themselves, "God is back, looking to the needs of his people!" The news of Jesus spread all through the country.

In many ways, this story reminds me of my mother-in-law, Dolores. In the 40-plus years I have known her she has lost her mother, father, brother, her husband, and her only child, my husband, Tom. Because she is 91 years-old, Dolores has outlived nearly everyone else in her extended family: aunts, uncles, cousins, and in-laws. She knows what it is to say good-bye, and she knows what it is like to be alone.

Yet, despite so much loss, my mother-in-law is not a quitter. She goes on her way, living life pretty much on her terms, relying on friends, faith and of course, her daughter-in-law and grandchildren. Dolores has a small income; and she is certainly not rich, but she does okay – far, far better than the widow we read about in our scripture this morning.

The widow of Nain is in truly desperate circumstances. A Jewish woman of this time and place has very few options to begin with. She is dependent upon her father's household until she marries and is then under her husband's care. After her husband's death, there is a possibility that one of her husband's brothers (if he had any) will marry her and care for her needs; but failing that, women like the widow in our story are wholly dependent on their sons for support.

Not only is the widow now without support, the death of her son means her home and all her possessions revert to her husband's family. In addition to losing her only child, the widow is now homeless, with no source of income, left with just the clothes on her back. She has literally lost everything. No wonder Jesus' heart breaks for her.

In Luke's gospel, Jesus has just finished the Sermon on the Plain, and has been healing and performing miracles. After this, Jesus and his disciples go on to Capernaum where some Jewish elders, speaking on behalf of a Roman centurion, approach them. The centurion begs Jesus to heal a beloved slave, and Jesus, "amazed" by the faith of a Gentile, heals the servant without ever seeing him. We can imagine the healing of this slave is like the middle picture in a triptych of Jesus' healing stories. Luke is now ready to move on to Jesus' next act of healing, this time in the city of Nain, about 35 miles southwest of Capernaum.

Jesus and his followers try entering the city gates of Nain, only to be pushed to one side by a crowd going in the opposite direction. The noise and wailing of mourners greets them as the crowd heads out of the gates on their way to the cemetery.

Unlike the previous healing story, no one in Nain rushes over to Jesus for help. Jesus sees the widow, but as far as Luke is concerned, she neither approaches Jesus nor speaks to him. Probably, she is keening the awful wail of a mother who has lost a child. Her heart is too broken and her eyes are too full of tears to notice others around her. Perhaps she is silent, in a fog of despair, helped along by sympathetic friends or neighbors. Maybe no one asks anything of Jesus because there is so clearly nothing to be done about the situation.

In any case, Jesus takes the initiative. Just as God breaks into our lives, Jesus inserts himself into this tragedy. His heart is broken at the sight of this mother, and he is filled with compassion for her. As happens throughout the gospels, Jesus' compassion leads to action. Not only that, Jesus walks calmly into a storm of broken rules. It is ritually unclean for a person to touch the dead, and touching a woman outside his family defiles a man. Jesus does not seem to notice.

In other healing stories, the crowd is quick to ask how the healed person had so sinned that he deserved his affliction. We remember when Jesus healed blind Bartimaeus the disciples asked if this man, blind from birth, committed a sin, or if it was through the sin of his parents. The ancient Near East saw ill health as the result of sin. Yet Jesus does not inquire, or even care to know this information about the widow or her dead son. Jesus offers unconditional compassion. He gives a great gift yet asks nothing of the recipient – not even to keep quiet about this miracle.

How many times in our lives have we faced a loss so great, so life altering that we throw ourselves on the mercy of God? How often have we bent God's ear with prayers and sighs too deep for words? How many times does it seem God is silent, either absent or uncaring, or perhaps for reasons we cannot fathom, the answer to our prayers is "no."

It might be of comfort to remember this story of Jesus and the widow of Nain. This widowed mother is of no consequence to the world, yet she is precious to God. Jesus, the human face of God, looks at her – not just with pity but also with the kind of compassion that draws him into her pain as if it were his own. He identifies with her and suffers with her on a gut level. Jesus is moved to perform a miracle, and restore her son to life.

Yet, for most of us, this kind of miracle never comes. It never came for my mother-in-law or countless others. Often, despite our prayers, this divine compassion seems to have passed us by. Why can Jesus not do for us what he does for the widow? The Revised Standard Version of Luke's text says that after Jesus brings the young man back to life, he gives him back to his mother. How we long for Jesus to give back to us those whom we lost!

Many years ago, Marcia, a woman in my home church, was forced to deal with the disappearance of her 20-year-old son. The young man left his place of work one afternoon and never returned. After a few days, his car was discovered in a forest preserve, but there was no trace of her son. There were no signs of struggle around the car – it was as if the young man simply vanished into thin air. The police suggested he might have taken his own life, but Marcia refused to believe it. "If he committed suicide," she said, "then why can't they find his body? How does a person bury themselves?"

Our church held a prayer vigil for Marcia and her son, and the minister made a point of saying that even though none of us knew where he had gone, God *did* know. No matter the circumstances of the young man's disappearance, God knew and God cared. One way or another, God was with him…or he was with God.

Many months later the young man's body was discovered in a deep ravine of the forest preserve and there was evidence he had indeed taken his own life. Yet, in the final chapter of this tragedy, God did give this son back to his mother. Not in the way anyone would ever want, but in truth, she now had him back. And not just back in the sense that his family could bury their child at last, but that in the end they had the full story of his life - from birth to death, the completeness, the wholeness of knowing the truth. As Christians, we know and hold fast to the truth of the resurrection. There will be a time when mother and son are reunited, never to be parted again.

If we wanted to make a movie about Marcia and her lost son, we would be sorely tempted to write an alternative ending – one in which God restores the son to life, just like the widow of Nain. Yet sometimes as we watch for God's miracles - God's special effects of life and death - we miss the minor miracles happening all around us. If we cling to the idea that miracles should always be like those in the New Testament, we risk not seeing the everyday miracle of God's compassion that enters a messy and pain-filled world to touch our most vulnerable places and restore our shattered hearts.

If we are looking for proof of this, we have only to remember our church is host to five AA groups. In fact, it would be hard to find a day of the week when an AA meeting is not taking place here. God is granting new life right here in our building! Lives are restored, hope is given, and those who are sometimes left for dead can rise again. When Jesus heals and gives new life, he does not bother to ask about the person's addictions or social status. When God restores, God does not care if it is in a church basement.

As a pastor, I have had many occasions to stand alongside a family in deep grief. As faithful and loving members of this church, so have you. Sometimes it is hard to find the right words to express to the family just how sorry we are for their loss. We are moved, as Jesus is moved, to have compassion for the widow, but one thing I cannot imagine myself saying to a bereaved family is what Jesus does in fact say: "Don't cry."

"Don't cry?" It makes no sense, and at the very least is pretty insensitive. Weeping is probably the only reasonable response. Before my husband Tom's death, I never knew what to say to a bereaved person. I was worried I would upset them by speaking about the person they had just lost. Would my presence remind them of their loved one and bring even more pain?

What I learned while Tom was ill and after he died was that those who talked about him were giving me a great gift. Their remembrances recalled not the pain of Tom's passing, but the joy of his memory. This compassion meant Tom was not forgotten, that he lived on in the memories of others as he did in our family.

A few months after Tom died I approached our family doctor. Jon delivered both our children and was a great support to our family while Tom was ill. I asked Jon if he remembered delivering Ashley and Ben. "Please tell me you do," I said, "even if you have to lie a little, because if you don't, then I'm the only one who remembers." I could not imagine being the only one left to remember something so important.

"Of course, I do!" said the man who by then had probably delivered hundreds of babies. "I remember it all."

Each one of us has the power to restore the dead to their loved ones by speaking about the person who has died. Nevertheless, it is tough because we must be willing to feel the loss, too. Just as Jesus' heart went out to the widow, so we too must hurt as the other hurts, because that is the essence of compassion. In this way, we give the deceased person back to their loved ones, if not in life, then at least in memory. Life may not be restored, but it is made real; it is tended and shared.

We know better than to expect supernatural, immediate healing. There may never be a cure. Yet, in walking alongside hurting people, listening and caring, healing can indeed happen. God is at work among us, and we are in a place of holy mystery.

In the name of the Father, the Son, and the Holy Spirit. Amen

Dashed Hopes to Burning Hearts
Luke 24:13-49

¹³Now on that same day two of them were going to a village called Emmaus, about seven miles from Jerusalem, ¹⁴and talking with each other about all these things that had happened. ¹⁵While they were talking and discussing, Jesus himself came near and went with them, ¹⁶but their eyes were kept from recognizing him. ¹⁷And he said to them, "What are you discussing with each other while you walk along?" They stood still, looking sad. ¹⁸Then one of them, whose name was Cleopas, answered him, "Are you the only stranger in Jerusalem who does not know the things that have taken place there in these days?" ¹⁹He asked them, "What things?" They replied, "The things about Jesus of Nazareth, who was a prophet mighty in deed and word before God and all the people, ²⁰and how our chief priests and leaders handed him over to be condemned to death and crucified him. ²¹But we had hoped that he was the one to redeem Israel. Yes, and besides all this, it is now the third day since these things took place. ²²Moreover, some women of our group astounded us. They were at the tomb early this morning, ²³and when they did not find his body there, they came back and told us that they had indeed seen a vision of angels who said that he was alive. ²⁴Some of those who were with us went to the tomb and found it just as the women had said; but they did not see him." ²⁵Then he said to them, "Oh, how foolish you are, and how slow of heart to believe all that the prophets have declared! ²⁶Was it not necessary that the Messiah should suffer these things and then enter into his glory?" ²⁷Then beginning with Moses and all the prophets, he interpreted to them the things about himself in all the scriptures. ²⁸As they came near the village to which they were going, he walked ahead as if he were going on. ²⁹But they urged him strongly, saying, "Stay with us, because it is almost evening and the day is now nearly over." So he went in to stay with them. ³⁰When he was at the table with them, he took bread, blessed and broke it, and gave it to them. ³¹Then their eyes were opened, and they recognized him; and he vanished from their sight. ³²They said to each other, "Were not our hearts burning within us while he was talking to us on the road, while he was opening the

scriptures to us?" ³³That same hour they got up and returned to Jerusalem; and they found the eleven and their companions gathered together. ³⁴They were saying, "The Lord has risen indeed, and he has appeared to Simon!" ³⁵Then they told what had happened on the road, and how he had been made known to them in the breaking of the bread.

³⁶While they were talking about this, Jesus himself stood among them and said to them, "Peace be with you." ³⁷They were startled and terrified, and thought that they were seeing a ghost. ³⁸He said to them, "Why are you frightened, and why do doubts arise in your hearts? ³⁹Look at my hands and my feet; see that it is I myself. Touch me and see; for a ghost does not have flesh and bones as you see that I have." ⁴⁰And when he had said this, he showed them his hands and his feet. ⁴¹While in their joy they were disbelieving and still wondering, he said to them, "Have you anything here to eat?" ⁴²They gave him a piece of broiled fish, ⁴³and he took it and ate in their presence. ⁴⁴Then he said to them, "These are my words that I spoke to you while I was still with you—that everything written about me in the law of Moses, the prophets, and the psalms must be fulfilled." ⁴⁵Then he opened their minds to understand the scriptures, ⁴⁶and he said to them, "Thus it is written, that the Messiah is to suffer and to rise from the dead on the third day, ⁴⁷and that repentance and forgiveness of sins is to be proclaimed in his name to all nations, beginning from Jerusalem. ⁴⁸You are witnesses of these things. ⁴⁹And see, I am sending upon you what my Father promised; so stay here in the city until you have been clothed with power from on high."

Three of the saddest words ever spoken are "We had hoped…" We had hoped the cancer was in remission. We had hoped our marriage could be saved. We had hoped our church would grow by now.

"We had hoped that Jesus was the one to redeem Israel."

Few things are more painful than dashed hopes. On the very day of Christ's resurrection Luke tells of two disciples on the road to Emmaus. They are going over the mad, rollercoaster ride of the last few days and weeks. Jesus – the one who was to redeem Israel – was instead brutally murdered. Women went to his tomb and found it empty…except for Christ's grave clothes, now transformed into angels.

Perhaps the full meaning of an empty tomb is blunted by hurt and disappointment. It is not just the tragedy of the last few days, it is also the enormous hole left behind of all the things that might have been. A great wound where there were once so many possibilities.

Where there is hope, there are also expectations. The disciples expected God would work in a certain way to save the world. They expected a warrior God, a mighty liberator king; but instead, they got a suffering servant. In our current context it is hard for us not to say, "I told you so." Or rather, "*Jesus* told you so."

How many times did Jesus tell his disciples about his ultimate fate? He taught from the prophets and the scriptures, yet they could not connect the dots about Jesus' resurrection. Well, I guess it often takes hindsight to understand that we were headed a certain way all along.

Most people prefer the future tense. It is much more comfortable to believe everything will be okay, or that all will go back to normal – and sooner rather than later, if you please. We like the future tense so much we sometimes short-circuit the process of dealing with the past. We shut a person down who wants to talk about their dashed hopes. Or perhaps it is ourselves we shut down and close off.

It was not until I prepared this sermon that I fully grasped the setting of this scene from scripture. Luke begins the passage with, "That very day…" The very day the women discover Jesus is not in his tomb, the morning Jesus appears to Mary, who runs to tell the other disciples. "Just before dawn, while it was still dark," Peter and the disciple whom Jesus loved run to the tomb and see for themselves. In other words, it is still Easter.

Yet for some reason, two disciples set out walking to Emmaus on what we think of as Easter afternoon. Well, no wonder they are discussing what happened earlier! Events still so fresh in their minds that they had yet to make any sense of them. Still, I wonder after all that transpired, why these two disciples just pick up and leave Jerusalem?

Perhaps they are frightened. As we learn in later passages, most of Jesus' other followers, terrified of what would happen next, hide out in a dark upper room. Would the authorities come for them next? After all, they are known associates of the crucified Jesus. "You are not also one of his disciples, are you Peter?" "Did I not see you in the garden with him?"

We can easily imagine how difficult it is for them to know what to do next. After all, there are very few Plan Bs for messianic revolutions.

In the absence of any real plan, two disciples default to what they know and understand. They go home; go back to work. Could these two disciples be heading to Emmaus so they can pick up where they left off before their journey with Jesus began?

A seven mile walk from Jerusalem to Emmaus. Time and space to transition from one version of life to another. It reminds me of that suspended moment just after my husband's death when I packed up his belongings in the hospital room, drove home, and made food, because it was dinner time and the children had to eat. We revert to the muscle memory of our old life.

When faced with the rubble of dashed hopes, some people, and I admit I am one of them, have an almost overwhelming urge to *flee*. Just get out of there. Leave the mess behind. Get on with it by getting away from it. Pretend it never happened at all.

Except, it did happen. Then, Jesus comes alongside and asks, "What are you talking about so earnestly while you're walking along?" This stops the disciples' conversation for a moment. They stand still, looking sad. Finally, Cleopas says, "Are you the only one around here who hasn't heard of these things?" And Jesus asks him, "What things? What things happened to you?"

Jesus and the disciples stop on the road and, before they try to journey on, Jesus stands with them and asks them to name their loss. He does the thing most essential to moving beyond grief: before he talks, before he explains, before he invites, Jesus comes alongside and listens.

If we want to follow the pattern set by Jesus, we will do likewise. For others, for ourselves, even for our church. Naming pain, grief, or loss helps us to transcend our dashed hopes so that they are no longer what defines us. After my husband died, my really *best* friends (not just the people I *thought* were friends) were the folks who patiently let me tell the story of his death over and over again, mostly without comment. These were the friends who allowed me to get to the place where I no longer mowed the lawn Tom's way, I mowed it *my* way.

This is not the same thing as erasing our memories, or even leaving them fully behind. It is an assurance of grace, and love, and promises. It is taking another crack at hope. Naming our dashed hopes helps us to create enough space to realize pain and fear are not the only reality. Faith teaches us it is okay to grieve the future that will never be, so we can embrace the future God has in mind. As someone once said, "When we have faith we are in a labyrinth not a maze."

It is also not about a means to an end. We cannot decide, "Well here you go: we've acknowledged the pain of the cross, so let's hurry up and go on to resurrection." None of us can do that because to be human is to be broken. Yet two flawed, brokenhearted disciples find the Risen Christ walking along with them even though they do not recognize him.

Really, truly accepting that Jesus is in our midst is disconcerting. When we gather for Sunday school, or worship, for a committee meeting, or fellowship meal - any time we come together to talk about Jesus or debate the future of our church - Jesus always comes and stands in the midst of us. We can never have a conversation about God, or Jesus, or the Holy Spirit without knowing we are speaking in their presence. The good news is that the God who has such intimate and comprehensive knowledge about us is also the loving God who never uses what we say against us.

We are free to name all "the things" standing between us and hope. We can acknowledge the reality of hurt and disappointment. There is no reason to keep the pain of grief to ourselves, nor run away from it.

As followers of Jesus, we must also offer others the grace of an unhurried ear. Before we talk, before we explain – certainly before we give advice, we invite hurting people to name their loss. This is what happens in a community of faith; we are a church *family*, after all.

I still wonder if we do enough talking and listening to each other about what we believe God wants for our church. In God's presence, speaking the truth in love, are we saying the things we need to say? Are there dashed hopes to be spoken aloud before we continue along the road God made for us?

I have been looking at photos of our church's past. I find myself looking at photos of a busy youth group, crowded pews, and many church activities that no longer happen. We know God has great plans for us, but sometimes we might need to talk about what we miss. It is hard to be truly excited about our future if we are still a little afraid in the present. "We had hoped…"

Yet when we name our grief, disappointment or fear in the safety of this place, and with the assurance of grace, we find these things have less of a hold on us than we thought, leaving us open to the surprise of God's decision to show up just where we least expect God to be.

Jesus walks this road with us, whether we notice him at first or not. There is only one person who truly knows what will happen in the future: the God who turns everything to his purpose; and God's purpose promises new life, second chances, forgiveness and grace for all — even when we are not paying attention.

Amen.

Get in the Boat
Mark 4:35-41

On that day, when evening had come, he said to them, "Let us go across to the other side." [36]*And leaving the crowd behind, they took him with them in the boat, just as he was. Other boats were with him.* [37]*A great windstorm arose, and the waves beat into the boat, so that the boat was already being swamped.* [38]*But he was in the stern, asleep on the cushion; and they woke him up and said to him, "Teacher, do you not care that we are perishing?"* [39]*He woke up and rebuked the wind, and said to the sea, "Peace! Be still!" Then the wind ceased, and there was a dead calm.* [40]*He said to them, "Why are you afraid? Have you still no faith?"* [41]*And they were filled with great awe and said to one another, "Who then is this, that even the wind and the sea obey him?"*

When I lived Chicago, Illinois, I thought I had it down about living next to Lake Michigan. All I had to do was drive east from the western suburb where I lived, and if I continued going east long enough I would eventually fall into the lake. (Just so you know, I never actually did that.)

Then I moved to the other side of the lake in Western Michigan. In the five years I lived there, I came to understand what it really means to live alongside Lake Michigan. Western Michigan has an entire "lake culture" with a beachy, boat-filled, water-centered vibe.

Actually, Lake Michigan is far larger than the Galilean lake — or *sea*, as Mark calls it in our scripture lesson this morning. If you have ever been to the Sea of Galilee, you know it is only a mile or two wide in some places. The Great Lakes, on the other hand, are visible from space.

However, that proximity does not mean the people of Jesus' time are cozy with the neighbors - far from it. The Sea of Galilee might be narrow, but it marks the dividing line between ritually "clean" and "unclean" populations. When

Jesus invites his disciples to "go across to the other side," they are setting sail for a place very different from the one they left.

Everywhere we look these days, we see images of refugees and immigrants getting into boats and sailing toward a future difficult for many of them to imagine. Struggling to escape the violence in their home countries, they pin their hopes and dreams – and very lives - on sailing to a better place. Many of them give their life savings to human traffickers who take the money, put too many refugees into much too tiny boats, and then disappear, leaving men, women and children to die at sea.

Even now, when the risks are well known, these disenfranchised people are so desperate to find a better life they continue to get in the boats. They know the dangers. They are less afraid to get into a leaky boat than they are to remain where they are.

Things are often no better for those who make it to the other shore. Receiving countries – especially Italy and Greece – simply cannot handle such a large influx of refugees. Authorities can only process so many people at a time, so thousands wait in detention camps, sometimes for years. Many must return to the desperation of their original circumstances where, given the opportunity, they would make the journey all over again.

Uncertainty lies ahead, but the refugees see no way forward without getting into a fragile, rickety boat. They know everything hinges on getting into that boat.

Jesus' disciples might know what awaits them on the other side of the lake, but on that calm clear day, they do not expect to almost drown getting there. Jesus does not give his disciples much choice but to "go across to the other side."

Jesus is coming off a long, hard day at the office, preaching to huge crowds about the kingdom of God. The crowd is so large in fact, Jesus is forced to climb into a boat and use it as a pulpit. The disciples must have anticipated the need to save Jesus from the crush of followers because they have a couple of boats all ready to go at the shoreline. When Jesus finishes preaching, it is nightfall, and like most exhausted preachers, he just wants to sleep. So, Jesus says to his disciples, "Let us go across to the other side."

Here is what Jesus does *not* say: he does not say, "I want to go to the other side, you stay here." Nor does he say, "You all go on to the other side; I'm tired so I'm not going with you."

Jesus does go with the disciples, and what happens next is the subject of many a Sunday school lesson, and countless works of art. Mark's story is one of the great miracle stories of the Gospels. Yet, we so often hear it out of context. We get one little snippet of the narrative and that can lead to a one-dimensional view of what Mark wants us to hear.

Mark tells us, "A great windstorm arose, and the waves beat into the boat, so that the boat was already being swamped. Yet, Jesus was in the stern, asleep on the cushion; and they woke him up and said to him, "Teacher, do you not care that we are perishing?"' He woke up and rebuked the wind, and said to the sea, 'Peace! Be still!' Then the wind ceased, and there was a dead calm."

Mark wants us to know God always hears our prayers, and no matter how stormy it gets, Jesus is in the boat with us. The earthly Jesus, exhausted and curled up in sleep, is the same divine Jesus who possesses the boundless power of

Almighty God. The disciples are awestruck. Mark writes, "'They say to one another, "Who then is this, that even the wind and the sea obey him?"'"

Jesus asks the questions he has repeated many times, "Why are you afraid? Have you still no faith?" No matter how rough the storms of our lives become, Jesus is always right there in the boat with us. We just need to remember our faith.

Now, I like this interpretation – I believe this interpretation is very real, very true. However, I also think Mark is calling us to an even richer understanding of the power of God in our lives.

First, we need to understand what is on the other side of the Sea of Galilee. This is the land of the Gerasenes. It is a Gentile region and the disciples know that. The Israelites and the Gentile Gerasenes are neighbors, and as such, I imagine they have some sort of trade agreement, or other interaction with one another. Still, that does not mean that after an encounter with the Gerasenes the Israelites do not come home and thoroughly wash their hands, letting out a sigh of relief because they are not like *those people*.

We know what the disciples have yet to learn: once Jesus brings his message across those geographic, cultural and religious boundaries, he will heal the most marginalized of all. Jesus heals a man who is so possessed by demons, so mentally ill, that his family can no longer control him. The man howls all night and cuts himself with sharp stones, so his people have no choice but to chain him out in the most unclean place possible: among the dead.

Yet Jesus heals this man and then – and this is the important part - sends him out to proclaim the good news of the Gospel in foreign lands. The Gerasene Demoniac was filled with hopelessness and sin. This formerly crazy, unclean man is the one chosen by Jesus to represent the kingdom of God to the Gentile world. Imagine that.

I wonder if the disciples would have balked at crossing over if they had known the whole story. What kind of Bible passage would we be reading if the disciples had said to Jesus, "Okay, but this boat isn't very sea-worthy in a storm – so, tell us if will there be a storm, okay?" Or if they had asked, "Well, first tell us *why* we have to go to the other side. That is an unclean land of unclean people. They are not like us!"

If Jesus had told them what to expect, I am very sure the disciples would have refused to get in the boat. "A violent storm, you say? A scary sort of miracle that calms the wind and waves? We are going to encounter a demon-possessed guy who lives in the cemetery? What do you mean you are going to send his demons into a herd of two thousand pigs? Then the pigs jump in the lake? Wait…what? This is a joke, right?"

We humans can do all sorts of brave things when we do not know the outcome, but the first step sometimes seems impossible. Sometimes, just getting in the boat with Jesus is the scariest thing of all. Even if we know we should do it, even if where we are is becoming unbearable, there is a certain amount of comfort in staying put… staying with our own kind. Not taking a risk that we will go through some inevitably stormy seas before we get to the other side. Not even taking a risk on people who make us uncomfortable.

Jesus calls us to get in the boat, even when we do not feel ready for the journey, because Jesus knows something about the other side when we do not. Human nature is such that, left to our own devices, we would rather stay where we are. We can ignore the need for change for a good long time, rather than start the process to make that change happen. Then Jesus comes along and says, "Why are you so afraid? Do you still have no faith?"

As individuals and as the church, we should understand that Jesus does not say, "There's nothing to be afraid of." Rather, he says, "Remember you have faith: faith in me and faith in my Father." Perhaps faith is what puts desperate people in tiny boats. Not because they are not scared, but because they have faith, and faith joins hands with hope.

The church has been sailing on some choppy seas for a while now. Yet, as communities of faith, we no longer have the luxury of staying on our side of the water. We can no longer think of those outside our comfort zone as "unclean." We can no longer deny them the same rights we enjoy. We are called to *have* faith and *share* faith across boundaries – boundaries that may challenge or even offend our religious institutions.

Sometimes getting in the boat is the hardest thing of all. Because that is the problem with Jesus: he is not satisfied with letting us live on our side of the lake for too long.

Getting in the boat with Jesus can be scary, because Jesus has the power to transform us, make us into something outside of, not only our comfort zones, but outside of our imaginations. If we wake Jesus up, he is going to start asking difficult questions about our faith and where it is leading us, questions we might not want to answer. Yet we must; and the place to start is by having the courage and the hope and the faith to *just get in the boat.*

Amen.

God Endures
Luke 21:5-19

⁵When some were speaking about the temple, how it was adorned with beautiful stones and gifts dedicated to God, he said, ⁶"As for these things that you see, the days will come when not one stone will be left upon another; all will be thrown down." ⁷They asked him, "Teacher, when will this be, and what will be the sign that this is about to take place?" ⁸And he said, "Beware that you are not led astray; for many will come in my name and say, 'I am he!' and, 'The time is near!' Do not go after them. ⁹When you hear of wars and insurrections, do not be terrified; for these things must take place first, but the end will not follow immediately." ¹⁰Then he said to them, "Nation will rise against nation, and kingdom against kingdom; ¹¹there will be great earthquakes, and in various places famines and plagues; and there will be dreadful portents and great signs from heaven. ¹²"But before all this occurs, they will arrest you and persecute you; they will hand you over to synagogues and prisons, and you will be brought before kings and governors because of my name. ¹³This will give you an opportunity to testify. ¹⁴So make up your minds not to prepare your defense in advance; ¹⁵for I will give you words and a wisdom that none of your opponents will be able to withstand or contradict. ¹⁶You will be betrayed even by parents and brothers, by relatives and friends; and they will put some of you to death. ¹⁷You will be hated by all because of my name. ¹⁸But not a hair of your head will perish. ¹⁹By your endurance you will gain your souls.

On Tuesday, November 8, 2016, the people of the United States voted for a new president. The results of this election will bring about a fundamental change in our country; one that will impact the entire world. Whether you consider this to be a good thing or a bad thing is up to you, but there is no denying we will never be the same again. I wonder if any of us are prepared for this. Is there truly any way anyone *can* be prepared for such a fundamental shift in the life and values of our country?

I do think most of us are so very weary of the way this election has played out in nastiness and fear that our overweening emotion is one of relief. We just want it to be over. We want to watch something on TV or read the paper, or go online and find something – anything! – not related to the American presidential election. If we never hear that phrase again it will be too soon.

Having said that, I imagine the last thing you want from your minister is for me to keep talking about the election, right? Yet, I believe not speaking about such a seismic shift in our lives is like ignoring the proverbial gorilla in the sanctuary this morning. There are excellent reasons why Presbyterians believe in the separation of Church and State. After all, you didn't call me to this church to be your political leader. I am here to point out where God is working in our lives, and in the life of the world. I am your pastor so that I can love and companion you as you walk the path of a faithful Christian, and seek to understand God's Word and will for us.

Some religious traditions love to use – some might say *misuse* – the Bible to score political points. We have all heard about TV preachers who point to natural disasters like tsunamis and hurricanes, or violence such as mass shootings as God's punishment visited upon those who do not hold the same beliefs as the TV preachers. This makes most mainline ministers want to, as Anne Lamott says, "Drink gin directly out of the cat's dish." That is not the same thing as following the famous words of theologian Karl Barth: "Take your Bible and take your newspaper, and read both. But interpret newspapers from your Bible."

We are called to respond to the world as people of faith. We should view all that happens through the lens of our Christian beliefs, and ask ourselves how God is at work in these events. How do we respond to the election results –

or really all that happens in the world – as Christ followers? Where we turn our gaze means everything if we ask ourselves if we are looking with Jesus' eyes.

In our scripture lesson for today, there is a definite disconnect between what Jesus sees and what the disciples see. Luke says Jesus and his disciples are admiring Solomon's astounding temple. Ancient writers tell us the temple of Jerusalem is massive, one estimate says 400,000 people could stand in it at the same time. Solomon built it to be the house of God for the ages. It is stunningly beautiful, adorned Luke says with "noble stones and offerings." The disciples ooh and awe. We imagine it is one of those settings where one cannot look around fast enough to take in the splendor.

Then Jesus bursts the disciples' bubble. "As for these things you see, the days will come when there shall not be left here one stone upon another that will not be thrown down."

As Luke wrote his gospel, Jesus' prediction was already fact: in 70 AD the great temple was utterly destroyed. The epitome of timeless magnificence was a heap of ruined stones.

The disciples are stunned and dismayed! Who? What? Where? When? What will be the sign that all this is coming? Yet, Jesus does not answer them directly. Instead, he warns the disciples to not be taken in by those who pretend to have all the answers. Someone is going to come along claiming to be the one person who can rescue us. "Do not follow them!" Jesus warns, "The people who tell you they will save you from ruin are in fact the very ones who will lead you to it."

For all the wonderful and honorable ways Americans go about electing a new leader, the very nature of the process tends to offer up those who consider themselves our country's savior. We are assured that if we just give this person our vote, they will solve all our problems - problems only they can solve. However, as Christians, we listen to these claims with different ears. We claim only one savior: our Lord Jesus Christ, and Jesus never made promises he did not keep. Instead, he placed his very body on the line for us.

In Luke's passage, Jesus is anything but smooth-talking and boastful. He tells the disciples there will be wars and insurrections, nation will rise up against nation, and the very earth will cry out in agony. Jesus' truth telling is painful, yet it is laced with the assurance of God's sovereignty and God's will to turn everything for the good.

"Don't assume these portends and disasters point to the end of time," Jesus tells the disciples. "Only God knows when the end will come, and even I can't say when that will be. Before God's kingdom finally breaks through, we will be faced with challenges, but these will lead to God's will for us." In Jesus' vision, dramatic historical events are the required stage setting for speaking God's truth.

The case may be made, that just like the mighty stones of Solomon's temple, the supports of our communal lives have been thrown down this election. Respect, decency, open mindedness, and honesty all appear to be in ruin. Still, as Jesus reminds his disciples, we are not only supported by God - who is our one true authority - we have an opportunity to testify to God's love. Jesus asks us to trust in the One who cannot be destroyed.

Jesus gives the disciples instructions on how to live and what to do in the meantime, difficult instructions to be sure, and ones that are just as challenging for us today. Yet, throughout it all, God remains faithful. The world is still broken, but the world is also full of God's grace and love. Just as it was over 2000 years ago, discipleship still means witnessing to our trust in God in the midst of circumstances that test our confidence and hope in a big way.

Secure in the knowledge of God's grace, we go on. We endure. We endure because God endures, and God never gives up on us. We let the world know we are believers in hope. God has done marvelous things – even when it looks otherwise.

We are called to have a vision that pierces through the present time to see a glimpse of God's plan for us. A good plan, one beyond anything we can imagine. We must witness to that even – especially – when it seems as if all things against God has gotten the upper hand. We endure, no matter what. Even if we feel ourselves paralyzed with grief, as I have felt myself post-election, Jesus says, "Your hardships will give you an opportunity to testify." That thought can cause many a Presbyterian to quake in their boots. We see ourselves as "head believers" before we are "heart believers." Testify? What does that look like?

Well, when Jesus was asked to distill down all the commandments – every important thing God has to say to us, this is what he said, "You shall love the Lord your God with all your heart, and with all your soul, and with all your mind. This is the greatest and first commandment. And the second is like it, you shall love your neighbor as yourself."

"Love your neighbor as yourself." We testify to God's love by welcoming the stranger, feeding and clothing the needy, and taking care of the marginalized because, as Jesus says, "just as you did it to one of the least of these…you did it to me."

We are commanded to love God with all our hearts, souls and minds; activities that do not leave much room in our lives for selfishness, bragging, or going after something we want at the expense of others. Today we can add racism, xenophobia, and misogyny to the list of things that have no place in our hearts, let alone in the kingdom of God. We witness to others by our commitment to sharing God's love, and working for the Lordship of Jesus Christ.

In her book, *Plan B: Further Thoughts on Faith*, Anne Lamott writes about calling a clergy friend during difficult times. "Where do we even start?" she asks. He replies, "We start by being kind. We breathe, we eat. We remember God is present wherever people suffer…we are never abandoned by God…it looked like Christ had been abandoned on the cross. It looked like a win for the Romans." "How do we help?" she asks him. "You take care of the suffering," he replies.

How then do we speak of God's love and faithfulness in our present climate? Jesus tells his disciples: "I will give you words and a wisdom that none of your opponents will be able to withstand or contradict." We need not worry about what to say, but speak up we must. In the words of Detrick Bonhoeffer, a theologian who died because he stood up to the Nazis, "We are not to simply bandage the wounds of victims beneath the wheels of injustice, we are to drive a spoke into the wheel itself."

It is crucial to let our lives speak God's truth. How? By showing respect and kindness to others, rising above destruction and despair, refuting pettiness and mean spiritedness, and working to better the world around us – even if we can only handle one small corner of it at a time.

We have hope in Christ. We endure because God endures. Because "Nothing in all creation will be able to separate us

from the love of God we have in Christ Jesus our Lord."
Amen.

Invisible Fence
Acts 11:1-18

11 Now the apostles and the believers[a] who were in Judea heard that the Gentiles had also accepted the word of God. ² So when Peter went up to Jerusalem, the circumcised believers[b] criticized him, ³ saying, "Why did you go to uncircumcised men and eat with them?" ⁴ Then Peter began to explain it to them, step by step, saying, ⁵ "I was in the city of Joppa praying, and in a trance I saw a vision. There was something like a large sheet coming down from heaven, being lowered by its four corners; and it came close to me. ⁶ As I looked at it closely I saw four-footed animals, beasts of prey, reptiles, and birds of the air. ⁷ I also heard a voice saying to me, 'Get up, Peter; kill and eat.' ⁸ But I replied, 'By no means, Lord; for nothing profane or unclean has ever entered my mouth.' ⁹ But a second time the voice answered from heaven, 'What God has made clean, you must not call profane.' ¹⁰ This happened three times; then everything was pulled up again to heaven. ¹¹ At that very moment three men, sent to me from Caesarea, arrived at the house where we were. ¹² The Spirit told me to go with them and not to make a distinction between them and us. These six brothers also accompanied me, and we entered the man's house. ¹³ He told us how he had seen the angel standing in his house and saying, 'Send to Joppa and bring Simon, who is called Peter; ¹⁴ he will give you a message by which you and your entire household will be saved.' ¹⁵ And as I began to speak, the Holy Spirit fell upon them just as it had upon us at the beginning. ¹⁶ And I remembered the word of the Lord, how he had said, 'John baptized with water, but you will be baptized with the Holy Spirit.' ¹⁷ If then God gave them the same gift that he gave us when we believed in the Lord Jesus Christ, who was I that I could hinder God?" ¹⁸ When they heard this, they were silenced. And they praised God, saying, "Then God has given even to the Gentiles the repentance that leads to life."

I have owned plenty of cats in my life – dogs, too. And even though our cats tried to persuade us otherwise, we have always kept them indoors. I can imagine scenarios with busy streets, fights with other cats or dogs, or even a hawk, and none of these scenarios end well. It seems to me, that cats who roam free have a shorter shelf life. Not to mention the fact cats kill songbirds.

Still, several years ago we had a black and white cat named Bailey. Baily was allowed outside under strict supervision. The cat knew his limits. We had drawn an invisible line around our backyard and front porch and Bailey was smart enough to know not to venture beyond it. He was also obedient enough to stay inside this line and come in when called. I guess you could say Bailey earned his outdoor privileges by sticking to the rules.

Now, I was under no illusions. I knew full well that Bailey Cat was perfectly capable of leaving his yard under certain circumstances. If Bailey had seen something really compelling – a mouse for example (Bailey *loved* to catch mice) - I knew he would forget his good manners and go after it. That's why I kept such a strict eye on him.

When I moved into my house in Tennessee, the previous owner showed me two dog collars and told me the house was equipped with an invisible fence. Her dogs wore these collars and if they tried to leave the yard, they would get a warning noise followed by a mildly unpleasant electric shock. You may have the same invisible fence system for your dogs. Dogs learn that it is very uncomfortable to try to cross the fence, and quickly understand their boundaries. I image we have all had the experience of walking past a yard where a dog has this kind of set up and discovered – as much as he growls and snaps, as much as he really, really wants to cross that fence – the dog will stay put. Crossing the invisible fence becomes repulsive to the dog.

In our passage from Acts, Peter is commanded by God to cross a line he finds repulsive and unthinkable. He is meditating on the roof of a house when he has a vision: a sheet lowered from heaven containing all the types of animals a good, observant Jew is forbidden to eat. In fact, I am not sure *anyone* would care to eat them! The blanket included creepy crawly things, vultures and other weird stuff you won't find me putting in *my* mouth.

Yet, God tells Peter to stand up, kill the animals and eat them. Peter is shocked. "By no means, Lord! I've been a good Jew all my life; nothing our laws call profane or unclean has ever passed my lips." Peter has a gut-level reaction, because this is what he has been trained to do all his life.

God gives an answer to this objection: "What God has made clean, you must not call profane." This exchange happens three times. Finally, Peter gets it: God alone gets to choose what is clean or unclean, acceptable or not acceptable. It is not up to us.

Peter's decision to keep kosher dietary laws and abide by Jewish taboos is grounded in deep faith. He undoubtedly spent a lifetime trying to remain ritually clean as a way of honoring God. That "no" to God was a visceral, reactive result from years of conditioning. Peter is not trying to defy God by crossing that boundary; it is God who has the power to redraw the boundary lines. It is not up to mortals to question God's decisions.

Peter is not given much time to contemplate what God is trying to show him with the blanket of forbidden food. When he relates it later, Peter's version of the story says three men show up on his doorstep "At that very moment." A soldier from Caesarea has sent three men from his household to Joppa, to the house where Peter was staying. The men are to fetch Peter back to Caesarea, and Peter experiences a strong urge from God's spirit to go with them.

Not only that, Peter is called to treat these non-Jewish strangers just as he would a fellow Jew. It seems a Gentile soldier named Cornelius found an angel standing in his house (what a shock that must have been!) and the angel delivered a message: "Send to Joppa and bring Simon, who is called Peter; he will give you a message by which you and your entire household will be saved."

Peter goes to Joppa, and sometime later, he is called on the carpet by the other apostles and fellow believers. He goes up to Jerusalem to explain why in the world he would have contact with uncircumcised Gentiles. To the Hebrew people of Peter's time, this is serious stuff. What one ate and with whom one ate it is only a small part of a very comprehensive code of law that regulated personal and community life. Mosaic Law covers every aspect of being human, from birth to death and all things in between; gender, health, jurisprudence, relationships, hygiene, behavior – and especially ethnicity, for non-Jews are automatically considered impure.

Here is the thing: instead of expressing the holiness of God, these laws could be misinterpreted. When this happened, it drew a fence around those who considered themselves close to God, and became a means of excluding people. Excluded people are considered dirty, polluted, contaminated, people Jews cannot imagine becoming close to, and certainly not people close to God.

So Peter is asked: "Why did you go to uncircumcised men and eat with them?" And Peter answers the question by telling his story. The author of Acts must consider this story so important that he tells it twice. Peter concludes by telling his listeners the Holy Spirit fell upon the people of Cornelius' household in the same way it fell upon all the disciples at Pentecost. "So," Peter says, "if God gave them the same gift that he gave us when we believed in the Lord Jesus Christ, who was I that I could hinder God?"

Who are *we* to hinder God? In the world today, people are great at justifying themselves, scapegoating others, and using God as an excuse for both. We draw sharp social boundaries, fences we would never dare to jump. Latino people are murders and rapists, Black people are lazy and criminally inclined, and the LGBTQ community is unacceptable to God, or anyone else for that matter. Oh, and women should know their place.

Peter found out God has a problem with that. God is not a God of partiality or favoritism. Jesus, to whom Peter gave his life, ignored, disregarded, and even outright demolished these distinctions of spiritual status. Theologian Marcus Borg writes that in place of the Leviticus passage, "be holy, for I am holy," Jesus deliberately substituted the call to be "merciful, just as your Father is merciful."

The Apostle Paul built on this in his letter to the Galatians, "In Christ there is neither Jew nor Greek, slave nor free, male or female." To those who would limit God's love to the morally upright, Matthew tells us God "makes his sun to rise on the evil and the good, and sends rain on the righteous and the unrighteous." Republican or Democrat, gay or straight, Christian or otherwise, wealthy or poor, every person is God's beloved offspring.

In his book, *Velvet Elvis*, bestselling author Rob Bell reminds us that the Christian gospel is good news about God's love to every human and all creation, "especially for those who don't believe it…The Church must stop thinking about everybody primarily in categories of in or out, saved or not, believer or nonbeliever. Besides the fact that these terms are offensive to those who are the 'un' and 'non' they work against Jesus' teaching about how we are to treat others."

Today, Protestant churches claim two things: we are an Easter people in a post-resurrection time, and we long to welcome more people into our churches. We have our eyes on what it means to be church today and tomorrow.

We can think of ourselves as the *insiders* God has chosen to go out into the world of outsiders to help them see the errors of their ways. Yet, the truth of the matter is that we are *all* outsiders who have been accepted and allowed in by the grace of a loving God.

All of us want to be God's insiders. Churches must be careful to not give those we think of as outsiders the impression that we have our own purity rituals in the form of traditions and habits. God calls us to do as Peter did, tell stories about God working in our lives. Tell stories about reconciliation, and tell them in humility and with a sense of urgency. Tell stories about our inclusive history. Stories that change the narrative about who is in and who is out.

I believe that, to a certain extent, mainline Protestant churches are hidden from the community. An increasingly secular culture is part of this scenario, and many churches contribute to it by not reaching out; reaching out to a community wounded by bad religion, or fear mongering, or a sense of unwelcome. If they only knew what we know: there are people here – right now - that are only too willing to jump the fence and embrace them – even if it means experiencing a mild shock. We need to share this good news boldly and with confidence in God's grace.

"Who am I that I could hinder God?" Peter asked the other apostles. They replied, "Surely God has given everyone the repentance that leads to life." And they praised God.

Let the people say, Amen.

Fearfully and Wonderfully Made
Psalm 139:1-6, 13-24

¹O LORD, you have searched me and known me.

²You know when I sit down and when I rise up; you discern my thoughts from far away.

³You search out my path and my lying down, and are acquainted with all my ways.

⁴Even before a word is on my tongue, O LORD, you know it completely.

⁵You hem me in, behind and before, and lay your hand upon me.

⁶Such knowledge is too wonderful for me; it is so high that I cannot attain it.

¹³For it was you who formed my inward parts; you knit me together in my mother's womb.

¹⁴I praise you, for I am fearfully and wonderfully made. Wonderful are your works; that I know very well.

¹⁵My frame was not hidden from you, when I was being made in secret, intricately woven in the depths of the earth.

¹⁶Your eyes beheld my unformed substance. In your book were written all the days that were formed for me, when none of them as yet existed.

¹⁷How weighty to me are your thoughts, O God! How vast is the sum of them!

¹⁸I try to count them—they are more than the sand; I come to the end—I am still with you.

²³Search me, O God, and know my heart; test me and know my thoughts.

²⁴See if there is any wicked way in me, and lead me in the way everlasting.

We have all been searched. At some point in our lives, like a sort of sea creature, the little shell of dignity where we keep the soft vulnerable bits of ourselves is breached. Sometimes this breach can be alarming or even devastating. Sometimes it can be exciting.

Perhaps it is when our beloved looks deep into our eyes, and sees the deepest level of our soul – or almost the deepest, because there are some parts of ourselves known only to us; or so we think. Then the relationship moves past the first blush of love, and enters that enduring phase where our spouse knows everything about us - good and bad. A single glance across a room filled with party-guests can communicate, "Isn't it about time to go? The babysitter is costing us a fortune."

There is something wonderful about being searched - and understood, and accepted.

Of course, there are the unlovely searches. You know this is true if you have ever gone through airport security. You have already taken off your jacket, shoes and belt, emptied your pockets, and placed your belongings on a conveyer belt. Still the bells and whistles go off! The contents of your luggage is riffled and inspected, and finally a TSA person takes you aside and frisks you to the point where you wonder if he shouldn't have bought you a drink first.

There is also that penetrating stare of a companion animal, the one that says, "I have seen you naked and never, EVER laughed. Now feed me."

It is a far different thing to be searched and known by God. It is wonderful. It is fearful. It is all encompassing.

"O LORD, you have searched me and known me. ²You know when I sit down and when I rise up; you discern my thoughts from far away. ³You search out my path and my lying down, and are acquainted with all my ways. Even before a word is on my tongue, O LORD, you know it completely."

If God knows and understand us like our best beloved, God also loves us like a parent. As a loving parent, Psalm 139 says, "God hems us in, behind and before and lays a hand on us."

The New Revised Standard Version of the Bible for our reading today is different from our pew Bible. The Revised Standard Version translates this passage as, "Thou dost *beset* me behind and before, and layest thy hand upon me." A loving mother does not "beset" a small child (unless that little person is about to run out into traffic), but she would walk before and behind, and keep a hand gently on the little head to guide and protect.

The hardest thing for us to understand may be the idea that God both searches us, yet at the same time, knowns every part of us. God searches, and at the same time is always *there* with us. Remember the story of Jacob who wrestles all night with an angel? In the morning, Jacob gets painfully to his feet, blinks in the morning light, looks around, and says, "Surely God is in this place and I didn't know it!"

God is in our deepest places; and most of the time, we do not really know it - or want to know it.

My experience of attending seminary was very different from what I expected. Actually, I didn't know what to expect, but it wasn't what I found. I felt as though seminary *excavated* me, so God could show me what I was really made of. I was an older student with a lot of life experience, so perhaps there were more layers and rocks and tree roots to go through until God could say, "Well, here are all the bits of you – good and bad. What will you keep, and what will you get rid of? And are you willing to listen to what *I* think?"

Actually, I could have dropped out of seminary, and there would still have been no way to escape this. I was *deconstructed*, but ultimately *reconstructed*, hopefully with a better idea of who God created me to be, and what God calls me to do.

It can be disconcerting to acknowledge God is always burrowing away in your life. Why does the God who created us continue to search for us? Perhaps because God gives us endless chances to choose him.

God is in our deepest places. This creator God is as mighty as the Big Bang and as tender as a crafter, carefully knitting us together, stich by stich. "My frame was not hidden from you, [God] when I was being made in secret, intricately woven in the depth of the earth."

Jeremiah 18:1-11 portrays God as a potter. Called by God, the prophet Jeremiah goes to a potter's house where the potter is working at his wheel. Jeremiah says, "The vessel [that the potter] was making of clay was spoiled in [his] hand, and he reworked it into another vessel, as seemed good to him."

God creates us, shapes and forms us, and loves us unconditionally. Like the potter's clay, we can become misshapen, but God preserves us and reworks us into a better, stronger vessel that God calls "very good." God shapes our beginnings and our endings, as well as every day in between.

God makes us and knows us. What a wonderful, *fearful* thing! Because if we are honest, we admit we don't really want to be known that well by *anyone* – even God. Where is the sense of control over life - control over the most intimate parts of our lives? We are startled to learn we can never truly get away from that. Sometimes we may resent it.

Our lectionary reading for today omits a few verses from Psalm 139, which I will include here. Verses 7 through 10 tell us:

[7]Where can I go from your Spirit? Or where can I flee from your presence?

[8]If I ascend to heaven, you are there; if I make my bed in Sheol, you are there.

[9]If I take the wings of the morning and settle at the farthest limits of the sea,

[10]even there your hand shall lead me, and your right hand shall hold me fast."

Methodist minister, David Troxler, writes: "It is a fearful thing to be known by God. We do not want to be known, but this searching, all-knowing God will not leave us alone. This God will not go away. We tried to kill him, and even that wouldn't work. Jesus just came back and said, "Lo, I am with you always, even to the end of the age."

Maybe the Revised Standard Version is right after all. Maybe the God who made us, searches and knows us does also "beset" us. God *besets* us and lays a hand on us. That sounds like God has laid siege to us, doesn't it? Imagine that! God besets us with love. God lays a hand on us and says, "You are my beloved child. I claim you."

C.S. Lewis once described his conversion to Christianity in terms of a long siege. He pictures God mounting a "steady, unrelenting approach," which Lewis has no desire to meet. "That which I greatly feared had at last come upon me. ... I gave in, and admitted that God was God, and knelt and prayed: perhaps, that night, the most dejected and reluctant convert in all England."

Yet Lewis goes on to offer thanks for the God of Psalm 139 when he says, "I did not then see what is now the most shining and obvious thing: The Divine humility which will accept a convert even on such terms... The hardness of God is kinder than the softness of men, and [God's] compulsion is our liberation."

What in the world do we do with this realization? The psalmist writes, "Such knowledge is too wonderful for me; it is so high that I cannot attain it." God's claim on us is something the human mind just cannot grasp. We will never know the mind of God, because our human powers of cognition will always be too limited. Just like Lewis, our only response must be surrender. *Sweet* surrender, because the battle is over, and we belong to the God who accepts all of who we are, and lovingly claims us despite our flaws. We are afraid to give everything up to God, only to find God gives us more than we can imagine. "How weighty to me are your thoughts, O God! How vast is the sum of them! I try to count them – they are more than the sand. I come to the end – I am still with you."

Surrender to God's persistence is sweet acknowledgement that God loves us unconditionally. God beheld us as an unformed substance and knew he would never let us go. It is a wonderful thing to be searched, to be known, to be besieged by this God. David Troxler writes, "Where can we go from [God's] Spirit? Where can we flee from your presence? Nowhere. Thank you, God. Search us then, and know our hearts. Test us and know our thoughts. See if there is any wicked way in us, and lead us in the way everlasting."

Thanks be to God. Amen.

Who Is the Greatest?
Mark 9:30-37

They went on from there and passed through Galilee. He did not want anyone to know it; ³¹for he was teaching his disciples, saying to them, "The Son of Man is to be betrayed into human hands, and they will kill him, and three days after being killed, he will rise again." ³²But they did not understand what he was saying and were afraid to ask him.

³³Then they came to Capernaum; and when he was in the house he asked them, "What were you arguing about on the way?" ³⁴But they were silent, for on the way they had argued with one another who was the greatest. ³⁵He sat down, called the twelve, and said to them, "Whoever wants to be first must be last of all and servant of all." ³⁶Then he took a little child and put it among them; and taking it in his arms, he said to them, ³⁷"Whoever welcomes one such child in my name welcomes me, and whoever welcomes me welcomes not me but the one who sent me."

It was one of the first children's sermons I gave as a new minister. I was seated on the chancel steps surrounded by a large group of kids ranging in age from toddlers to third graders. In most ways, it was a typical children's message. I brought something to show the kids: an object lesson for the older ones and something to focus on for the very littlest. I was asking questions and the children were answering, when a quiet ripple of laughter fluttered through the congregation. I look a quick look at the kids, but for the most part, they were focused on our conversation. Then came some rustling to my right, which quickly bloomed into shuffling and thudding and by this time the grownups were laughing out loud.

Well, it seems Henry – a three-year-old blond, angelic-looking stick of dynamite – had taken exception to something a neighboring three-year-old boy had whispered and, in response, Henry landed a punch. The other boy pushed back, and Henry dragged his opponent behind the communion table for some rolling and kicking.

To those seated in the pews, it was like that scene in the Wizard of Oz when the Cowardly Lion, Tin Man and Scarecrow battle the Wicked Witch's henchmen behind some rocks. Nothing to see but noise and dust until every once in a while, an arm or leg (or tail) shoots out.

The next moment Henry's mother – who sang in the choir and could see all the action – sprang from her seat, swooped down on the two boys and hauled them out of the sanctuary, one little arm gripped in each hand. I do not think their feet actually touched the ground on the way out.

Children's sermons are like that: expect the unexpected. For grown-ups, watching these adorable little rabble-rousers is charming. In our society, we honor childhood as something almost sacred. In our communities, children are loved and respected as persons, allowed time to learn and grow into the adults they were created to be.

Of course, there are tragic exceptions: children in desperate need, those who are mistreated, or are victims of the horrors of human trafficking. Yet, in our modern, privileged, Western world, our view of childhood is almost romantic. It is light years away from the way it was in Jesus' day.

In our text for today, Jesus calls to a child of the household where he and the disciples are staying. Perhaps the child is a servant, half-hidden behind a curtain, invisible to adults until called to perform a task. Jesus gently calls the child to him, and wrapping his arms around the little one, places her in the midst of the disciples.

In our current context, we cannot *begin* to understand what a shocking, radical thing Jesus did. Here stands a group of male adults - the privileged age and gender - and into this gathering Jesus inserts a *non-person*. That is the status of a child in antiquity: a socially invisible non-person.

Scholars of that day wrote very little about childhood. Even ancient medical writing shows no real interest in kids. A male baby is celebrated at birth because he represents status for his mother and security in his parents' old age. Historically, childless Roman citizens who needed heirs were more likely to adopt adults rather than children. In another scripture passage, the disciples shoo children away from Jesus as if they were a pack of mongrel dogs. Jesus quickly instructs them: "let the little children come to me."

How utterly shocking it is, then, when Jesus scoops up a child, gives the child pride of place among the disciples, and tells them this non-person is a stand-in for Jesus! The disciples must have been speechless; shocked into silence at such a thought.

Those disciples were certainly not silent on the road through Galilee. Some Bible translations say they were arguing. The Revised Standard Version says they were discussing. The disciples were discussing, Mark writes, who was the greatest. Jesus had just told them, "The Son of Man is going to be betrayed into the hands of men. They will kill him, and after three days he will rise." Mark tells us the disciples did not understand Jesus' words. Maybe this declaration was more than they could handle. Were they in denial? Were they too afraid, as Mark says, to ask questions? In any event, the disciples change the subject.

Well, Jesus may have appeared oblivious to the discussion, or argument, but he knew what the disciples were saying. Still, he wants to hear it from them. "What were you arguing about on the road?" Nobody raises a hand.

Jesus sits down. This is symbolic of his status as a teacher. Unlike today, teachers in ancient times sat and students stood. Maybe Jesus takes a seat because the disciples, with their foolish and petty talk, just make him tired.

Mark says the disciples were "discussing with one another who was the greatest." Reading this passage, it reminds me of when my son was a little boy. You see, I never had any brothers, so when Ben had friends over to play, I heard what sounded to me like nothing but boasting and put-downs. I wondered if I should go in there and break things up; tell them they were being mean. However, if you are a man, or a woman with brothers or sons, you know I was wrong. Playful rivalry is how little boys relate to one another! It's a guy thing.

Let us cut the disciples some slack and assume they were engaging in a game of one-ups-man-ship to pass the time on a long road. Perhaps the quicker of the disciples have taken in more of what Jesus taught than it seems. Maybe they understood what Jesus told them after all. Although, I cannot imagine the disciples understand his words about resurrection.

In the disciples' minds, Jesus is the new king who is going lead Israel out of Roman oppression. Jesus is also the Christ, the chosen one of God, who knows how to predict his own death. If Jesus is going to die, someone has to take over the leadership position. It just makes sense. Perhaps the disciples were arguing about qualifications for that position.

Someone must assume a leadership role. We understand what that means: the headman will sit at the top of the table, make policy decisions, and issue orders; all the while being served by those who are lesser-than. It works that way in the corporate world, doesn't it?

Jesus says it does not work that way in the Kingdom of God. If our calling as Christians is to work for the Kingdom while we wait for Jesus to come again, it should not work that way for us, either.

Look, we know in today's world the rich are getting richer and the poor are becoming even more desperately poor. If one has achieved something – even if it is an infamous something – one brags about it. Our politicians sound a lot like those little boys I spoke of: nothing but boasting and put-downs. As Christians, we are called to a different way of life. Jesus says if anyone would be first, that person must be last of all and servant of all.

We could say Jesus is not so interested in who we *say* is the greatest, or which person *acts* like the greatest or strives to *be* great. Jesus is interested in who acts with the greatest grace, the greatest compassion, and the greatest love.

So what does this mean for the Church? Especially churches that long to live deeply into God's calling as transformative agents of peace and healing in the world. We must be willing (and no one says it will be easy) to embody a sense of radical hospitality. We must adopt new practices that call us to think differently about our church.

Jesus emphasizes the relationship between welcome and greatness. His message is, if you want to be great, you must celebrate and welcome others in unconditional love, especially those who can benefit you the least. This kind of welcome is possible only when we see God in others.

Jesus took a child - a non-important person, a non-person, and centered that child in the middle of the disciples. I have to think the disciples reflexively took a step back, so that the child on the margins is now the center of their concern. What Jesus was trying to make clear to them is the vital importance of moving outsiders *inside*. Saying to his disciples: welcome is the truly greatest thing.

Reformed churches today are sort of hovering in mid-air…waiting. Waiting to see if the Protestant church is going to grow or disappear. The question is how do we grow and thrive as the church of Jesus Christ while hovering and waiting to see what will happen?

The answer, of course, is that we cannot. Yet in this time of rejecting those we see as different - different colored skin, different sexuality, differently abled - we are selecting ourselves as "the greatest." Heavens, the last thing any of us want to be is the greatest racist or misogynist.

Our beautiful churches are sitting empty. What would happen if the people we invite to join us are the people sitting on the margins of society? The non-persons.

Jesus says, "Whoever receives one such person in my name receives me; and whoever receives me, receives not me but him who sent me."

Amen.

Open Hearts, Willing Spirits
Acts 16:9-15

During the night Paul had a vision: there stood a man of Macedonia pleading with him and saying, "Come over to Macedonia and help us." ¹⁰When he had seen the vision, we immediately tried to cross over to Macedonia, being convinced that God had called us to proclaim the good news to them. ¹¹We set sail from Troas and took a straight course to Samothrace, the following day to Neapolis, ¹²and from there to Philippi, which is a leading city of the district of Macedonia and a Roman colony. We remained in this city for some days. ¹³On the Sabbath day we went outside the gate by the river, where we supposed there was a place of prayer; and we sat down and spoke to the women who had gathered there. ¹⁴A certain woman named Lydia, a worshiper of God, was listening to us; she was from the city of Thyatira and a dealer in purple cloth. The Lord opened her heart to listen eagerly to what was said by Paul. ¹⁵When she and her household were baptized, she urged us, saying, "If you have judged me to be faithful to the Lord, come and stay at my home." And she prevailed upon us.

What was I thinking? There I was, the single mother of a ten-year-old and a soon-to-be thirteen-year-old, working for an advertising agency, and I had just plunked down serious money to go on a trip overseas to Greece and Turkey. Doug and Susan, the pastor of my church and his wife were leading a tour following in the footsteps of the Apostle Paul's second mission trip. I had been reading about this trip for weeks in our church newsletter, but one day for some unknown reason, I filled out the form, wrote a check for the down payment and dropped it off at the church before I could change my mind. What was I thinking?

One thing I knew for sure: I was not in a particularly good place in my life. I had ended a relationship that could kindly be called "disastrous," and I was not happy cranking out advertising copy about financial services. I felt stuck.

What do you imagine Paul was thinking when he awoke the next morning after a dream in which a man from Macedonia pleads with him to come there and help? After all, Paul and his companions have a mission trip all planned out, and it did not include Macedonia at all. Paul planned to travel to Asia, but the Holy Spirit turned him away.

Now, this location is not Asia as we think of it today, but rather a Roman colony in Asia Minor. Paul and his fellow travelers, Timothy and Silas, tried to go there twice only to be stopped by the "Holy Spirit of Jesus." Scripture does not tell us how exactly the Holy Spirit prevented Paul from going to Asia. Did travel arrangements breakdown? Was there a lack of funds? Did word come that this part of the world was too dangerous? Somehow, Paul and Silas stall out in Troas. Sometimes the Spirit of God can be so subtle we only notice what is happening later when we begin to put all the puzzle pieces together.

Quakers have an excellent expression for times when life's doors keep slamming shut on us. They call it "way closing." There is also the expression, "way opening," for times when plans are firmly and repeatedly denied us, yet something unexpected happens. Often, "way opening" leads us in a direction we had no intention of taking. Yet, if our hearts are open, this unexpected path can become an unexpected gift.

Personally, I have a pattern of repeatedly smacking into a brick wall before I stop and look for where the Holy Spirit is providing a way open and out. Part of spiritual formation for any of us is to gradually learn to keep listening for God's still, small voice, even – especially – when we are being led in a direction we have never considered. This takes practice.

Yet, that is the way the Lord seems to work: proving once again that the mind of God is greater than anything we can conceive. I might think I have the perfect plan, or I might be stuck; empty of any plan at all; yet God has other ideas. Those ideas inevitably lead to something much greater than I could possibly imagine.

Perhaps Paul was frustrated when his plans to evangelize Asia were derailed. Yet, Paul has a history of God breaking into his life in a rather spectacular fashion. Once a Pharisee bent on destroying the nascent Jesus cult in Damascus, Paul is thrown to the ground by God, blinded, and commanded to change his life.

So when Paul converted to Christianity and devoted his life to God, he also learned the more subtle art of discerning a call from the Holy Spirit. Very few of us will ever experience a slam-to-the-ground, lightning-and-thunder call from God. It is so much subtler than that. Listening for the Spirit working in your life takes time and practice, and a certain amount of life experience. Most of all, discernment takes a willing heart.

Many people go through a "way closing" time in their professional life. One's work is no longer satisfying, and instead has become stressful. Doors that were supposed to opened shut instead. The problem for most of us is that when all the doors have slammed shut behind us, it is often too dark to find a way forward. With doors closed behind us, and our noses pressed firmly against a brick wall, it can feel as though we have nowhere to go. Yet somewhere in that dark place, God is offering us a gift. The way forward may not be clear, but God, who is our loving parent and wants us to have abundant life, offers us time and space to think and pray about what we really want. Sometimes this might seem self-indulgent, especially if we have responsibilities in life. In my opinion, it is best to process through this time with neutral, professional guidance. The very most important thing is to take the time you need to explore what means most in your life, reassured by the knowledge that God wants only the best for you. As Parker Palmer writes, "The deepest vocational question is not 'what ought I to do with my life?' It is the more elemental and demanding, 'Who am I? What is my nature?'" To that I would add, "What brings me joy?"

Paul literally dreams about his way forward. Although plans were set for Asia, Paul immediately turns his eyes toward Macedonia. The man in Paul's dream never states what help is needed, but under the circumstances, Paul believes he is being called to proclaim Christ in what we today consider Europe. It was the first-ever Christian mission trip to that part of the world; something in all likelihood Paul never considered doing before.

First, Paul and Silas spend a few days in the seaside city of Philippi. On the Sabbath, they do what is a pattern for Paul's missionary trips: they look around for the nearest synagogue. The local synagogue is a place to pray, and provides a chance to meet fellow Jews and talk to them about Jesus. Our scripture reading tells us only that a place of prayer is outside the city gates. Synagogue? House Church? Coffee shop? New churches start in unlikely places. There, Paul and Silas encounter a group of women who are also there to worship and pray. As we read on, all sorts of remarkable things happen.

Paul (former persecutor of Christians) sits down with these women. Paul takes a seat, the traditional posture of a teacher, and speaks to women – not men – about Christ. Among his listeners is Lydia of Thyatira who is a dealer in purple cloth.

Lydia is unusual in a number of ways. First, she is an independent business owner at a time when women are little more than property. Not only that, Lydia deals in purple cloth, a very costly commodity reserved for the elite customer; and she is the head of a large household. Not only is Lydia wealthy and influential, she is also a seeker after Christ. "The Lord opened her heart to listen eagerly to what was said by Paul" verse 14 tells us, and she is baptized along with her entire household.

Lydia invites Silas and Paul to her home, "If you have judged me to be faithful to the Lord, come to my house and stay." Lydia is not a woman to be refused. Not only do Paul and Silas enjoy her hospitality, they return later to stay with Lydia when they leave prison. Although she might not have thought of it in just this way, Lydia becomes Europe's first leader of a house church.

Paul is thwarted in his attempt to evangelize Asia by the grace of God. By the grace of God, he goes to a Roman province in Europe, where he encounters a group of people he should have never met. By God's grace, a businesswoman from Thyatira is interrupted in prayer outside the gates of Philippi. Paul and his companions traveled straight through Thyatira on their way to Macedonia, yet the Holy Spirit led them all the way to Philippi to meet Lydia. Whatever Lydia was thinking that day, it was most likely not that she was to become one of the founding mothers of Christianity in Europe.

Whatever possessed me to sign up for that trip to Greece, God's grace led me to the site of ancient Philippi, where there is still a river for baptism. I have told the story of re-affirming my baptism in those ancient waters, and how God's spirit spoke to me in a completely unexpected way. I knew nothing more than God claimed me, and realized God had been doing so all along, even when I did not know it. God loved me, just as every one of us is loved. I knew without a doubt, then, that I was God's person; I just did not know what to make of it. By the grace of God, I had stalled out in my life. By the Holy Spirit, I was led to sign up for a trip I never intended to take, where I heard the words that would send my life in a completely different direction.

It is important to note that I spent many years after that day in Philippi trying to discern what God was calling me to be and do. I did not hop off the plane from Greece and run to the nearest seminary. That was my call. *Your* call can be something entirely different. The vital thing to remember is that we are all called by God's spirit to live an *abundant life*. As theologian Frederick Buechner famously wrote, "God calls you to the place where your deep gladness and the world's deep hunger meet."

Being human means doors are going to slam shut on us. Those are our "way closings," and most times these "way closings" are a blessing from God, because they stop us long enough to listen to our lives.

We are given time to ask God some questions, such as, how are you speaking to me now, and what are you saying? What do you want me to take with me as I walk my faith journey, and what should I leave behind? What can I learn from these closed doors?

May God richly bless you as you discern the answers, no matter where you are on your faith journey.

In the name of the Father, and of the Son, and of the Holy Spirit.

Amen.

Putting on Christ
Romans 13:8-14

⁸Owe no one anything, except to love one another; for the one who loves another has fulfilled the law. ⁹The commandments, "You shall not commit adultery; You shall not murder; You shall not steal; You shall not covet"; and any other commandment, are summed up in this word, "Love your neighbor as yourself." ¹⁰Love does no wrong to a neighbor; therefore, love is the fulfilling of the law.

¹¹Besides this, you know what time it is, how it is now the moment for you to wake from sleep. For salvation is nearer to us now than when we became believers; ¹²the night is far gone, the day is near. Let us then lay aside the works of darkness and put on the armor of light; ¹³let us live honorably as in the day, not in reveling and drunkenness, not in debauchery and licentiousness, not in quarreling and jealousy. ¹⁴Instead, put on the Lord Jesus Christ, and make no provision for the flesh, to gratify its desires.

When I was a little girl, I loved to play dress-up. My mother kept a box of old clothes, including, bless her heart, her college formals. I now cringe to think of how we treated those custom-made gowns from the 1930s! The box also contained old hats, gloves, and costume jewelry. I would spend hours in the backyard putting on those too-large clothes and then terrorizing the little boy next door into joining me as we pretended to be grown-ups.

I can also remember slipping my feet into my dad's dress shoes. I would put on one, and then the other, and then look down to see what a tiny amount of space my little feet used up inside those, to me anyway, *huge* shoes. I would try to shuffle forward, but I always ended up either stepping right out of the shoes, or else falling flat on my face.

In Western cultures at least, we do not expect children to take on adult roles until they have had time to grow and mature. Even if they are wearing adult clothes and pretending to be grown-ups, no one expects them to have grown-up minds, or to behave as adults. Even small children know about make-believe. Play is the process of transitioning into adulthood; it gives kids a chance to dream big about who and what they will be in the future.

Kids should act like kids, but inside every child is a kernel of *possibility*. With loving assistance, we anticipate children will grow into not just our expectations for them but, more importantly, become the people God created them to be.

In our scripture for today, the apostle Paul offers advice to the young church in Rome as they grow into a mature congregation. He begins by reframing God's commandments in light of Jesus' teaching. Although Paul does not cite Matthew's gospel, he reminds the church of how Jesus replied to Jewish scholars and officials who tried to trip him up on the Law of Moses.

We can picture the crowd close to Jesus, one of them pushing forward one of the officials who is an expert on the Law. The official begins with false deference saying: "Teacher, since you say you are the Son of God, you must know God's favorite commandment. So let's hear it – which is the greatest commandment of the Law?"

Jesus replies: "Love the Lord your God with all your heart and with all your soul and with all your mind…and the second [commandment] is like it: Love your neighbor as yourself. All of the law hangs on these two commandments."

All of the law hangs on loving God and loving neighbor.

Paul tells the church in Rome that the commandments to love God and love neighbor not only sum up all the rest of the Law, they actually fulfill it. If you love God and love neighbor, you are putting into practice all Ten Commandments.

Some days, keeping God's commandments might seem like a do-able project, a cosmic to-do list: No, I have not killed anyone – check. No, I have not stolen anything…no, I have not committed adultery – check and check. Keeping the Sabbath, hmmm…Okay, not a perfect score but I *am* trying. Yet, when Jesus and later, Paul – tell us that every item on the checklist hangs on loving neighbor as oneself, we start to believe an overwhelming task has been set before us.

Yet the law can bring us the good news of the gospel. We cannot separate gospel from the Mosaic Law. It seems as if some people believe the Bible begins and ends with the New Testament, and that Jesus comes to replace the Law. (Jesus has something to say about that.) Maybe they think this lets them off the hook. Thank you, Jesus! Yet, we cannot privilege the New Testament over the Hebrew Bible. God's commandments are an invitation to love God and neighbor, and if that is not the gospel message then I do not know what is.

Reading Paul's letter reminds us that the Ten Commandments can be broken down into two sections: how to have a relationship with God, and how to have a relationship with others. The first three commandments: to have no other God, to worship God and not make an idol of anything else, and to use God's name with respect and honor, lays out how to live with God. The fourth commandment, to remember the Sabbath day and keep it holy, is a bridge between how to live with God and how to live with our neighbors. We honor God by keeping the Sabbath, and we set aside a day that honors the image of God in each one of us.

This way of thinking helps us to see the full story of the cross. We live upwards toward God and, at the same time, we love outward toward one another. Paul's message to the Roman church simplifies these ways of living with God and neighbor. Offer to your neighbor the best intentions you have for yourself. He condenses it down so they have something solid to remember.

If it feels overwhelming to be faithful to God every day, acting out love for neighbor, every day, remember this - we are called to clothe ourselves in the Lord Jesus Christ.

Like playing dress-up, these "clothes" are much too big for us. God's love is more sovereign, more vast and mighty than anything in our limited, human imagination. Yet God knows that inside of every one of us is a kernel of *possibility*. Paul says, "Stretch and grow into Christ's expectations for you."

Paul writes, "Love does no harm to a neighbor." That, to me, sounds like the Hippocratic Oath – "First do no harm." If we are honest, we should admit the impossibility of actually loving everyone we meet. Still, starting from a place where we do them no *harm* is a seismic step forward. First, do no harm. Let us pray that those in power get this message. Change is inevitable, but harm does not need to be part of it. Paul asks us to view love as a behavior, rather than as an abstract emotion.

In Paul's day, Christians believed Christ's coming and the fulfillment of God's kingdom were close at hand. He encourages the Roman church to "understand the present time: to know the hour has already come for you to wake up from your slumber, because our salvation is nearer now than when we first believed. The night is nearly over; the day is almost here."

This is not the time to nod off or take anything for granted, Paul advises. Wrap yourself in Christ, and put on a protective layer of goodness and honesty. This is not playing dress-up, but creating total congruence between what you do in both public and private. If there are parts of your life that shame you, places where you are not proud of what you have done to others, or even to yourself, remember you will one day meet Christ. Behave always as if someone was shining a searchlight on you.

Millennium later, Christians still live in hope of Christ's return. We believe the world's new day dawned with Jesus Christ, and ever since his resurrection, the world is caught in the overlap between old and new. Each day should be lived as if Christ's second coming is right around the corner. In the Romans passage, Paul was speaking of eschatology – end-times. Just as we cannot predict the "new heaven and new earth," neither can fragile, mortal, finite humans say when our own individual "end-times" will come. As it was when we were children, we live simultaneously in the now and the not yet. Just as our parents knew, God knows that within us there are always possibilities. We *can* love God with everything we have. We *can* love others as ourselves. Yet right now, those possibilities hang on us loosely, and it is our job as Christians to grow into them through Jesus Christ.

Love is the greatest identity marker of any Christian, and of any Christian community. Loving God and loving neighbor should be our norm, our fixed point. Because of what God has done, is doing, and will do for us in the future through Christ, we can live with the possibility of genuinely transformed lives. We can dress-up in Christ and become new persons who love our neighbors as we love ourselves. Our faith in Jesus Christ allows us to put on shoes that are much too big for us without stumbling and falling flat on our faces.

Paul said, "Whoever loves others fulfills the law." Every day holds a new possibility to fulfill the law in this way. We have a new opportunity to say, "I love you" - loudly, and with full intention.

Amen.

Hold Fast to Hope
Hebrews 10:11-25

[11] And every priest stands day after day at his service, offering again and again the same sacrifices that can never take away sins. [12] But when Christ had offered for all time a single sacrifice for sins, "he sat down at the right hand of God," [13] and since then has been waiting "until his enemies would be made a footstool for his feet." [14] For by a single offering he has perfected for all time those who are sanctified. [15] And the Holy Spirit also testifies to us, for after saying, [16] "This is the covenant that I will make with them after those days, says the Lord: I will put my laws in their hearts, and I will write them on their minds," [17] he also adds, "I will remember their sins and their lawless deeds no more." [18] Where there is forgiveness of these, there is no longer any offering for sin.

[19] Therefore, my friends, since we have confidence to enter the sanctuary by the blood of Jesus, [20] by the new and living way that he opened for us through the curtain (that is, through his flesh), [21] and since we have a great priest over the house of God, [22] let us approach with a true heart in full assurance of faith, with our hearts sprinkled clean from an evil conscience and our bodies washed with pure water. [23] Let us hold fast to the confession of our hope without wavering, for he who has promised is faithful. [24] And let us consider how to provoke one another to love and good deeds, [25] not neglecting to meet together, as is the habit of some, but encouraging one another, and all the more as you see the Day approaching.

Imagine something with me. A retired minister is writing a letter to one of his former churches. Many years earlier, when the minister was a young pastor, he helped plant this church along with several other churches, and has been closely associated with the good folks there ever since. That pastor is now semi-retired, but still doing missionary work, and the news from his old church is disconcerting.

Many of the same wonderful parishioners are still active members, but they are not as young as they used to be. Through a combination of disenchantment with the way things are done, and the aging and passing of many faithful members, the church is decidedly in decline.

After all, it is not as if the surrounding culture offers much support for the Christian life these days. Much of the younger generation no longer attend church, and the same few members are trying to carry on the church's mission by themselves. Not only that, every time they hear the news it seems as if evil not only persists in the world, but the world is getting too discouraged to push back against it. The minister is frankly worried for this congregation.

All sorts of ideas pop into the preacher's mind. Maybe this church needs the razzle-dazzle of a praise band! Or perhaps they could enter a float in the next 4th of July parade – you know - get the young people real excited about what's going on in church… He quickly dismisses those ideas, picturing the congregation struggling through unfamiliar music or trying valiantly to scramble up a ladder onto a flimsy float. He downs a couple of aspirin and tries again.

The minister thinks he has a pretty good grasp of the problem. The people are so discouraged they do not have the energy for growth. They don't come to church so they can't experience the deep love and encouragement offered by their fellow members. Maybe, the pastor thinks, maybe what the church needs is to remember what Jesus Christ did for them. Really, truly, deeply remember and discover afresh the wonder of hope in the Lord. The what, and the why, and the who of Christ's sacrifice should lift up their eyes to the prize and keep them there. The minister picks up his pen and writes:

Dear Brothers and Sisters in Christ Jesus, every priest goes to work at the altar each day, offers the same old sacrifices year in, year out, and never makes a dent in the sin problem. As a priest, Christ made a single sacrifice for sins, and that was it! Then he sat down right beside God and waited for his enemies to cave in. It was a perfect sacrifice by a perfect person to perfect some very imperfect people. By that single offering, he did everything that needed to be done for everyone who takes part in the purifying process. The Holy Spirit confirms this:

"This new plan I'm making with Israel
  isn't going to be written on paper,
  isn't going to be chiseled in stone;
this time "I'm writing out the plan in them,
  carving it on the lining of their hearts.

I'll forever wipe the slate clean of their sins. Once sins are taken care of for good, there is no longer any need to offer sacrifices for them. So friends, we can now—without hesitation—walk right up to God, into "the Holy Place." Jesus has cleared the way by the blood of his sacrifice, acting as our priest before God. The "curtain" into God's presence is his body.

*So let's **do** it—full of belief, confident that we're presentable inside and out. Let us keep a firm grip on the promises that keep us going. He always keeps his word. Let's see how inventive we can be in encouraging love and helping out, not avoiding worshiping together as some do but spurring each other on, especially as we see the Big Day approaching.*

Yours in Christ,

Paul

Well, as some of you will recognize, Paul's letter is the same Hebrew passage we read earlier, but the translation is from Eugene Peterson's, The Message. You probably also understand Paul's concerns for the early church are not necessarily ancient history. We see this same scenario playing out today. Paul's church seems to be in need of hearing again the basic elements of Christian faith – and most importantly – they could use a refresher course on what it means to have hope in Jesus Christ.

It is all too easy to look at the surrounding culture and forget Jesus' sacrifice was a once-and-for-all-time, crushing blow to sin and evil. Sin and evil are still a daily fact of life. If people of the early church had problems remembering that, imagine what they would think about the worst attack on Paris since the Second World War? What in the world would those people say when a gunman slaughters 20 little children and 6 brave teachers? How would they react to dire poverty in an age of abundance, or violence against women and children? Actually, I don't think we have to work very hard to know how they would feel. Because it is how you and I feel right now. Discouraged…angry…frustrated…and I am sure you can think of many other emotions as well. The emotion hardest to conjure up in this climate is hope.

The book of Hebrews tells us God has implanted God's reign of hope and forgiveness right inside our hearts; no need to be constantly wondering and worrying whether or not we have it right, and certainly no excuse to judge the salvation of others. Jesus gave us a once-and-forever ritual cleansing so we now have the confidence to approach God at will, knowing we are forgiven and loved, knowing God craves a relationship with us. So if all is well, why does the world seem oh so wrong? Where is hope found?

No wonder so many younger people question the necessity of attending church. On the surface of things, there seems to be no compelling reason to be part of something that does not appear to be working. When we speak to them of hope, they hear hypocrisy, because the outside world does not jibe with what is going on inside here. Warily, younger people ask why it is we want them to worship with us – is it just a cover-up for asking for money? Sadly, if one never spends time as part of a congregation, one never experiences the love, acceptance, and care waiting for them in abundance. There is a sad circle of not knowing what one is missing and therefore not being willing to look for it within the doors of a mainline church.

If Jesus broke the back of sin and evil, why is there still suffering? We know Christ has defeated evil, and is sitting at God's right hand; but the completion of his battle is still in progress. Christians are people who live simultaneously in the *now* and the *not yet*.

There is a story about a missionary family in the 1960s, called to serve in a remote part of Africa - father, mother, and three young children. Now, that part of Africa was known for extremely large, extremely dangerous snakes. For all I know, it still is. It would be nothing for a snake of that size to wrap its coils around a small child, or even an adult, and squeeze the life out of them.

One day the missionary family returned to their humble house to find that one of these horrific snakes had gotten inside. The mother and father quickly sent the children outside and the mother ran to the nearest neighbor for help. Now, this was a good neighbor to have, for the man was a native villager, well acquainted with these snakes and what to do about them. He told the mother and father to go outside with the children and stay there until he had killed the snake by chopping off its head with a machete.

"Now this is important," the villager said gravely to the family, "No one is to go back into the house until I give the all clear – *no matter what!* Do you understand?" Well, the family understood, so they waited as their neighbor went back into the house to kill the snake. First, they heard a loud *whump* as the machete came down on the snake. They were about to breathe a sigh of relief when suddenly there was a terrific noise coming from inside. Splintering of glass, crashing and breaking, even thuds against the walls! The noise went on and on and the family was terrified. Amid the sounds of crashing and breaking, their neighbor came out of the house. He said, "Please stay out until after the noise stops. Wait a long time, longer than you think you have to. That snake is as dangerous dead as he is alive."

The family was puzzled. Their neighbor explained: the snake's head was cut off, but his body had yet to recognize the fact. The snake's huge body was still thrashing wildly – spattering blood all over the wrecked house. The snake was defeated, you see, but the snake would not realize that for a sometime to come.

Through the grace of God, through the saving death of Jesus Christ, evil has been defeated, but evil does not know it is dead yet. It is still dangerous, still creating blood and havoc, and will be so until Christ comes again. Through Christ, we know sin, and death, and evil have been wiped out, and through faith, we live in hope until Christ comes again. Evil is over, but it is not done with us just yet.

As author and preacher Thomas Long writes: "If you want to know the truth, pay more attention to the gospel you hear than to the obsolete evil you see, thrashing in its death throes in the world."

Today, we celebrate the gifts God has given us, including the gift of worshipping as free and forgiven people. In turn, we show our gratitude to God by offering what we can to this church. We know a pledge card is not the same thing as paying a bill or making a payment. A pledge card is a symbol of hope. Hope that is patient in dark times, and hope that embraces the other without judgement, hope that opens the door to all who seek the kingdom of God.

Amen.

Salt and Light
Matthew 5:13-20

"You are the salt of the earth; but if salt has lost its taste, how can its saltiness be restored? It is no longer good for anything, but is thrown out and trampled underfoot. ¹⁴*"You are the light of the world. A city built on a hill cannot be hid.* ¹⁵*No one after lighting a lamp puts it under the bushel basket, but on the lampstand, and it gives light to all in the house.* ¹⁶*In the same way, let your light shine before others, so that they may see your good works and give glory to your Father in heaven.*

¹⁷*"Do not think that I have come to abolish the law or the prophets; I have come not to abolish but to fulfill.* ¹⁸*For truly I tell you, until heaven and earth pass away, not one letter, not one stroke of a letter, will pass from the law until all is accomplished.* ¹⁹*Therefore, whoever breaks one of the least of these commandments, and teaches others to do the same, will be called least in the kingdom of heaven; but whoever does them and teaches them will be called great in the kingdom of heaven.* ²⁰*For I tell you, unless your righteousness exceeds that of the scribes and Pharisees, you will never enter the kingdom of heaven."*

Reformed faith traditions sometimes have a tendency to intellectualize our beliefs. One day Jesus walks into a Presbyterian church and asks the congregation the same question he once asked his disciples: "Who do you say I am?"

Well, the congregation looks at the minister, the minister looks at the session, the session looks back at the minister and finally the minister answers Jesus. "You are the eschatological manifestation of the ground of our being, the kerygma in which we find the ultimate meaning of our interpersonal relationship with God."

And Jesus says, "What?"

Jesus prefers plain talk, and he likes to tell it straight. In our scripture reading this morning, Jesus continues the Sermon on the Mount by telling his listeners who and what they are. "You are the salt of the earth. You are the light of the world." In other words, this is who Jesus says we are.

Notice that Jesus is not saying, "You *should* be the salt of the earth and the light of the world," or, you *must* be, *or else*. Rather Jesus says you *are*; you already are salt and light to the world. This is what Jesus knows to be true about us, even when we do not believe it or forget we ever knew it.

To be followers of Jesus requires Christians to live a certain way and do what Jesus calls us to do. Yet, what we so often forget is that this is as much a promise as it is a command. Not only that, the promise – the blessing – always *precedes* the command. God gives us the gift of life, and mercy, and love, and then asks us to respond to those great blessings.

We receive grace, and are to reflect that grace back into the community by the way we treat others. As St. John of the Cross wrote, "The followers of Jesus are to be windows through which the divine light enters the world."

Jesus and his followers lived life in accordance with the Law of Moses. Jewish religious leaders of that time taught that God's demands are fulfilled by very specific and precise actions and observances. Jesus calls his disciples to look beyond the rules to find God's original intention - to be in relationship with people who obey from the heart, people who obey God, not because they are afraid of punishment, or hope they will be rewarded in some way, but rather because God's mercy and grace changed their hearts. They cannot keep from rejoicing and sharing this grace with others.

God's grace precedes God's call. This grace and love create an identity for us; one that is truer and more generous than anything the world offers or observes. Think back over the last couple of weeks, and take a moment to remember the ways God has used you to be salt and light. Could it be the encouragement you offered, or the faithful work you performed, the prayers you prayed, or the protest you made.

This may be hard because, after all, we are raised not to brag, and are taught to walk humbly with God. But recalling those times when you "let your light shine" also reminds us that all we do in love reflects back, not on us, but on the God who gave us those good gifts in the first place.

Still, what does Jesus mean when he calls us "salt and light"? In our world salt is a natural seasoning that - in moderate amounts - is necessary for balanced nutrition. We take it for granted; after all, what is as ubiquitous as common table salt? Is Jesus saying we are boring and predictable?

Remember though, in Jesus' time, salt was very valuable. It not only gave flavor to food, it also was used as a preservative in the days before refrigeration. We might very well see our role in today's culture as one of preservation. A pervasive sense of fear and uneasiness fills our world, and perhaps we are called to hold up the banner of hope in such a discouraging climate. We preserve the message of the gospel in a world that seems to have forgotten Jesus altogether.

It is also clear there is confusion about what such a banner looks like, and who has the right to lift it. However, we should never underestimate the importance of the church being a place where all viewpoints are respected. Perhaps congregations are called to gather those who may differ in the understanding of what it means to be salt and light, but are committed to pray for one another, and to ask God for wisdom and courage.

In Jesus' time, salt was so prized it could be used as currency. Special salt rations were given to Roman soldiers, known as *salarium argentum* – the forerunner of the word "salary." Even today, it is a compliment to be considered "worth your salt."

Yet Jesus warns, "If salt has lost its taste, how can its saltiness be restored? It is no longer good for anything, but is thrown out and trampled underfoot." Well, those of you who paid attention in high school chemistry know salt – sodium chloride – is a very stable element and technically can never lose its flavor. The only way salt loses its taste is if it is so diluted or dispersed, it becomes unnoticeable.

It is tricky for an individual or a congregation to find that balance between a faith that overpowers and shames, and one that is reduced to a well-known cliché about being "spiritual but not religious." We are the salt of the earth when we are valuable, stable, preserving, but without either deficiency or excess.

And as it is with salt, so it is with light. To be called the light of the world by Jesus is no small thing. We all remember singing, "This little light of mine, I'm gonna let it shine…" Yet it seems to me that if we are to light the world "this *little* light" is not going to cut it. We need a great *big* light.

In Jesus' day, a lamp was a small clay vessel about the size of your hand. Oil is poured in the bottom, and a piece of fabric soaked in oil is poked through a little opening where it is lit. Even unlit it is easy to see it really will not give off much light all by itself. So you can imagine what would happen if we hid it under a basket.

Yet, Christ tells us that even a small light can shine boldly if we use it to illuminate the good done to help others and point to God. If we try to hide our little lights, to keep them just for ourselves, they cannot do the job God intended for them to do. Keeping them close, rather than placing them where all can see, turns us inward and leaves the world just as dark as we first found it. Unfortunately, many leaders today tell us we should keep any light to ourselves, and ignore the needs of the world.

On the other hand, even small lights, when grouped together, can shine big time. Rather than just illuminate our own personal faith journeys, we are called to join together to "let our light shine before men." It is not meant to be stored up and enshrined, but rather to be shared with all who need its guidance and warmth.

Martin Niemoeller was a German minister during the time of Hitler and the Nazis. For years, Niemoeller held on to the hope that the German government would eventually emerge from its self-created darkness. When it did not, he felt he must openly oppose what the government was doing, which led to his arrest. Right before his arrest, Martin Niemoeller spoke about Jesus' words: *you are the light of the world*. He said:

"It is in these days that I realized – I understood – what the Lord Jesus Christ means when he says: 'Do not take up the bushel! I have not lit the candle for you to put it under the bushel, in order to protect it from the wind. Away with the bushel! The light should be placed on a candlestick...We are not to worry whether the light is extinguished or not, that is God's concern. We are only to see that the light is not hidden away. Let your light shine before men! The city of God will stand, because its strength comes from on high."

Because we belong to God, we are already the salt of the earth, and no loving God would ever trample us underfoot. As followers of Jesus, we are called to love as God loves, and to insist the world does not trample on anyone else, either. Because God loves us, we are light to the world. Because God lights the lamp, our job is to let our light so shine, regardless of the world's attempt to extinguish it.

We experience amazing grace in God's gift of love and community and new life, and we want to reflect that grace in the way we relate to others. We let our light so shine before others because God's grace changed our hearts, and we can do no less.

Amen.

What Do You Want God to Do for You?
Mark 10:46-52

⁴⁶They came to Jericho. As he and his disciples and a large crowd were leaving Jericho, Bartimaeus son of Timaeus, a blind beggar, was sitting by the roadside. ⁴⁷When he heard that it was Jesus of Nazareth, he began to shout out and say, "Jesus, Son of David, have mercy on me!" ⁴⁸Many sternly ordered him to be quiet, but he cried out even more loudly, "Son of David, have mercy on me!" ⁴⁹Jesus stood still and said, "Call him here." And they called the blind man, saying to him, "Take heart; get up, he is calling you." ⁵⁰So throwing off his cloak, he sprang up and came to Jesus. ⁵¹Then Jesus said to him, "What do you want me to do for you?" The blind man said to him, "My teacher, let me see again." ⁵²Jesus said to him, "Go; your faith has made you well." Immediately he regained his sight and followed him on the way.

"Jesus, Son of David, have mercy on me!"

At the mention of Jesus' name, Blind Bartimaeus lifts his head and cries out from the deepest, most desperate part of his being. Perhaps it was his last chance. He is swept up in a crowd that believes Jesus is the Anointed One of God, and with the crowd, he trails after Jesus, hoping for a show of miracles.

Bartimaeus must have been quite loud to be heard above the noise of this rabble. After all, profound need and desperation call us to reach out boldly in ways we might not have previously thought possible. For many people, dark times solidify our faith. Faith is a welcome intrusion on misery, appearing out of nowhere when there seems to be no hope. Sometimes God needs our broken places to enter into our hearts in a new way.

Even people of faith sometimes flounder in darkness. Sometimes that broken place comes at us out of the blue, from a world of hate, or an onslaught of illness or despair; a slam of bad luck or poor decision-making. Other times, we are in prisons of our own making – not because we are sinners, or chose to be miserable, but because we have come to believe the worst about ourselves. Upbringing, circumstance, or depression teach us we are unlovable, and we buy into that program of self-doubt or self-loathing.

About twenty years ago, my life seemed to hit rock bottom. I thought it had reached bottom several times before – only to find a lower level of bottom I did not know was there. Each time I found myself asking, as Dorothy Parker wrote, "What fresh hell is this?"

One snowy winter night I could not sleep. It was probably that witching hour of 3:00 a.m. What is it about 3:00 a.m.? I was so disheartened and discouraged, so knocked flat and devoid of any belief in myself, I could not imagine a time when I was not in this dark place. To make matters worse, I was convinced – by myself and by others with their own agendas – that all of it was my fault.

I was bored with crying in bed, so I wrapped myself in a blanket, grabbed a box of tissues, and went downstairs to cry on the couch. At least it was a change of scenery. After a while, when I was finally out of tears, I sat silently watching snow falling outside the window.

That was when it happened.

If something like this has ever happened to you, you know what I mean. I heard a rich, warm voice – whether it was a voice in my head or a voice aloud, I will never know. The voice said, "I love you exactly as you are." With the voice came a great peace that seemed to roll over me like enveloping cloud. I was dumbstruck, yet unafraid.

Later, I told my spiritual director about this, saying, "I *think* I heard God's voice." She paused and asked, "Why would you believe otherwise?"

When we cry out to God in pain or desperation – whether we are aware we are crying out or not, it is seldom pretty or, as they say on Public Broadcasting, suited for "more sensitive viewers." Faith is needy, faith is raw; it is impetuous and risky. Faith is about God doing something we cannot do for ourselves, God doing exactly what we need in a particular moment, often when we ourselves do not know what we need.

Our scripture lesson from Mark begins from a place of darkness and need. Jesus and his disciples are passing through Jericho. In Mark's lean and urgent style, they are in and out of Jericho in two sentences, yet manage to collect a crowd of followers. When Jesus and his disciples and the crowd of followers reach the city gates, they find the usual group of beggars waiting for enough charity to make it through one more day.

These are the lowest of the low. If we think we have problems, we should remember that these folks had everything against them. In the ancient Near East, beggars are both physically dirty and ritually unclean. No decent person would come near them. These people really have nothing to lose; they are well beyond the margins of society, they are at rock bottom.

Maybe that is why the blind beggar Bartimaeus – the one whose name means "Son of Honor" – cries out so loudly and insistently to Jesus. His faith emboldens him. Faith, after all, is not only risky, it is also hopeful. For blind

Bartimaeus, hope – in the form of Jesus Christ – is passing by on the street right in front of him, and he seizes the opportunity.

Bartimaeus hears the whispers and gasps that Jesus the Anointed One is headed out the city gates and he begins to shout: "Jesus, Son of David, have mercy on me!" The crowd –especially Jesus' disciples – is appalled. This man is doing everything wrong! People living on the margins are supposed be ashamed and keep their mouths shut! Human nature is such that we choose to filter out the sight and sound, and smell, of those who fit our definition of outsiders. How dare Bartimaeus address the Son of God at all, never mind with a raucous shout?

Not only that, but as a matter of practicality Bartimaeus is calling attention to himself and all the other Jews on the street that day. When you are a Roman-occupied population, you do not want to do that, because it never ends well. The crowd shushes him. I imagine the disciples are especially embarrassed by the scene this man is causing. Even Bartimaeus' fellow beggars would have told him to pipe down. Yet, nothing deters him. He shouts even louder: "Son of David, have mercy on me!"

There is something about this part of the gospel story that always goes straight to my heart, and just rips around in there. It is like the cry of the man whose son Jesus healed of an evil spirit: "I believe – help my unbelief!" Somehow, these from-the-gut cries hit a chord of need and remembrance and raw emotion that can bring tears to our eyes. Is there any one of us that has not cried out to God for mercy; we believe, but we have no idea where to go from there?

Jesus stopped and said to his disciples, "Call him."

Then everyone – in a teacher's pet sort of way – begins calling out to Bartimaeus. "Hey, you there, cheer up! Take heart! This is your lucky day, Man! You better stand up because Jesus is calling you." In two words: "Call him," Jesus moves Bartimaeus away from the margins and into society; from being an outsider, to being an insider; and all this *before* Jesus heals him. What a miracle it is when we simply acknowledge the outsider's presence, when we call them into the human circle.

Bartimaeus throws his cloak aside, jumps to his feet and comes to Jesus. How did he get there? After all, he is blind. Does someone, emboldened by Jesus' action, touch an untouchable person, take his elbow and guide him over to the Lord? Now the crowd is not just witnesses to mercy, they are among the merciful. The breakthrough has begun.

Jesus asks an interesting question. He looks at Bartimaeus and inquirers, "What do you want me to do for you?" Questions like this open a conversation and they can begin a relationship. How often has someone given you what he or she thinks you want, without even asking if it is what you want – or need? I think we can assume the Son of God knows what Bartimaeus needs, but Jesus gives him the dignity of making that choice for himself. Bartimaeus replies, "My teacher! I want to see!"

When he casts aside his cloak, Bartimaeus is throwing aside every meager thing he has in the world. With this act, he gives up even the pretense of having possessions. He also frees himself for a larger faith. Like people who leap from mountainsides with no parachute, Bartimaeus is in free-fall. What must that be like? What is this hurtling descent like for us cool and careful and decently ordered Christians? Could you – or *have* you - stepped off the edge of space led by an all-or-nothing need to see Jesus?

Jesus said to Bartimaeus, "Go; your faith has made you well." Unlike the carefully stepped procedure Jesus used to cure another blind man, Bartimaeus, in one of Marks' favorite expressions, *immediately* has his sight. Also unlike other recipients of Jesus' miraculous healing, Bartimaeus stays with Jesus and follows him on the way to Jerusalem. How could Bartimaeus know he was following Jesus into Jesus' own darkness and death? Without any evidence to support my viewpoint, I want to believe Bartimaeus stayed with Jesus from his triumphal entry into Jerusalem all the way to the cross.

What do you need Jesus to do for you? An equally important question to ask is what does Jesus want *you* to do? Jesus already knows want you need, whether or not you cry aloud like Bartimaeus. Even if we do not need to hit rock bottom before we know God loves us, it is still important to keep our eyes wide open to the merciful face of Jesus.

I am convinced we each need to cast aside our cloaks as we walk toward Jesus. This cloak may be a symbol of our self-loathing or our despair. Just as likely, it might represent our sense of self-sufficiency or pride. Either way, God hears us. We may never be healed, but by the grace of God, we can be made whole.

I would like to ask you to take some time this week to consider what you would do if *hope*, in the form of a loving Savior, walked past you on the street. Would you dare shout out a confession of faith: "Jesus, Son of David, have mercy on me! Jesus, Son of God, I believe, help my unbelief!" Would you risk it? What would hold you back from seizing an opportunity like that? As Paul tells us, "Nothing in all creation will be able to separate us from the love of God in Christ Jesus our Lord."

As followers of Jesus, Christians are called to watch out for those on the margins and to hear their cries. To see them as a child of God, beloved just as you are beloved. They need us to at least *see* them, and affirm them, and perhaps even guide them toward Jesus, to be loved and be healed.

Please pray with me in the words of St. Francis:

"O Lord, make me an instrument of Thy Peace!
Where there is hatred, let me sow love.
Where there is injury, pardon.
Where there is discord, harmony.
Where there is doubt, faith.
Where there is despair, hope.
Where there is darkness, light.
Where there is sorrow, joy."

Amen.

More Than We Know
Matthew 13:31-33, 44-52

[31] He put before them another parable: "The kingdom of heaven is like a mustard seed that someone took and sowed in his field; [32] it is the smallest of all the seeds, but when it has grown it is the greatest of shrubs and becomes a tree, so that the birds of the air come and make nests in its branches." [33] He told them another parable: "The kingdom of heaven is like yeast that a woman took and mixed in with three measures of flour until all of it was leavened."

[44] "The kingdom of heaven is like treasure hidden in a field, which someone found and hid; then in his joy he goes and sells all that he has and buys that field. [45] "Again, the kingdom of heaven is like a merchant in search of fine pearls; [46] on finding one pearl of great value, he went and sold all that he had and bought it. [47] "Again, the kingdom of heaven is like a net that was thrown into the sea and caught fish of every kind; [48] when it was full, they drew it ashore, sat down, and put the good into baskets but threw out the bad. [49] So it will be at the end of the age. The angels will come out and separate the evil from the righteous [50] and throw them into the furnace of fire, where there will be weeping and gnashing of teeth. [51] "Have you understood all this?" They answered, "Yes." [52] And he said to them, "Therefore every scribe who has been trained for the kingdom of heaven is like the master of a household who brings out of his treasure what is new and what is old."

Poet Emily Dickenson famously advised, "Tell the truth but tell it slant." Poetry has a way of coming at us sideways as it goes beyond our minds and straight into our hearts. We can say the same thing about parables. Jesus' parables can be frustrating, never giving us a straightforward account, but instead "tells it to us slant" in surprising ways. A way that catches us off guard, and slips right on past our logical right brain.

Parables are kind of like a biblical "earworm," if you have ever heard the term. Instead of songs that get into our heads and refuse to go away, Jesus' stories rattle around our subconscious until they begin to make sense. In my opinion, Jesus uses parables that stick with us until his teachings take root in the deepest parts of our lives.

In our scripture reading this morning, Jesus hits his listeners with a barrage of parables to describe God's kingdom, both in the present, and at the end of the age. Actually, "describe" is not really the right word. Jesus wants to *evoke a response* to the ways God unexpectedly breaks into our lives. As Celtic Spirituality would say, we are to see God in all things, and as Reformed theology would say, we are to respond to God's gift of unearned grace.

Did you learn the parable of the mustard seed in Sunday school? Our teachers taught us that, even if we have faith only as tiny as a mustard seed, God grows that faith as large as a great big tree. Apparently, God does not need much to work with.

When I was in Sunday school, it was something of a status symbol for little girls to own a necklace with a real mustard seed incased in plastic. I never asked my parents for one. Somehow, it did not seem right to display my "little" faith because that was between God and me. It seemed like bragging. Goodness, even as a six-year-old Methodist I was a good little Presbyterian, wasn't I?

As I learned later, wearing a mustard seed necklace is actually like hanging a piece of kudzu around your neck. In Jesus' time, mustard plants were pernicious weeds. Farmers dread them because they take over a field and, as Jesus says, create a home for birds. What farmer wants something growing in his field that attracts birds?

The folks listening to Jesus would have a similar reaction to the story of a woman who hid leaven in three measures of flour. Leaven would render the flour useless. It is a rotting, molding lump of bread, and three measures of flour would make enough bread to feed 100 people. So, the woman would basically ruin her enormous batch of bread and have to throw it all out at Sabbath.

Is the kingdom of God like nasty weeds hiding in a bag of good seed? Does God's kingdom include an act of corruption? If we tell it slant, we might notice that in Jesus' parable, God is present and at work in our everyday lives – whether we see that or not. Planting crops or baking bread, God is there, powerfully. Weeds and moldy bread aside, the hidden side of God's kingdom is far more potent than anything we can imagine. It might look like a spore or tiny seed, but the kingdom of God is alive and active in the present moment.

No matter how bad life looks to us, God turns evil into something good and grace-filled. Maybe not right under our noses, but it will happen. God's good creation might be obscured by evil, but evil will never erase the image of God within what God created.

Being surprised by God, as C.S. Lewis wrote, is being surprised by *joy*. "The kingdom of God," Jesus taught, "is like treasure hidden in a field, which a man found and covered up; then in his joy he goes and sells all that he has and buys that field." In the same way, we can imagine the weary merchant who has spent years collecting pearls, only to be surprised by joy when he finds a pearl beyond value. A common field; an ordinary marketplace. What God does when we are not paying attention!

God blesses us with unexpected love and grace. Grace we are too broken and limited to deserve. We are as unruly as weeds in a garden, and we are as destructive as mold in bread, but God loves us anyway. Clear away the mess we can make of ourselves, and discover we have contained treasure all along. As John Wesley wrote, "There is within every human heart a treasure God has placed."

We hear in Jesus' story of hidden treasure and a priceless pearl something more: a call to respond. Parables surprise us with the way God's kingdom breaks into the reality of our lives. They invite us to feel deep down what it is to glimpse God's work in our lives and in the world, and to respond in gratitude.

In the story of the man who discovers treasure in a field, the treasure is not as important as how the man responds. In order to buy the field, he sells everything; all his possessions, anything he has of value. Receiving the treasure God wants to give us is an all-or- nothing proposition, and taking hold of God's promises involves our whole person. Searching for meaning in your life is impossible when you are only prepared to go half way.

Gaining something wonderfully unexpected can be more satisfying than anything we imagine. Perhaps the merchant was ready to retire, maybe sell off his inventory so he could have a little money to live on. He has a vision for the future that, while not very exciting, seems pretty good to him. We can imagine the merchant regularly prays to God for a terrific sale, one that would keep his family going for months. Yet, as far as the merchant is concerned, God never answers his prayer, at least in the way the merchant wants it.

I am sure the man – on an ordinary day, in an ordinary market place – never thought of finding a priceless pearl. Yet God has plans for him beyond his wildest dreams. Thankfully, the merchant knows value when he sees it, and leaves the modest pearls behind.

I have a bad habit of treating God like a short-order cook. I know what I need, and I know when I need it – usually *right now* – and I like to tell God exactly how to go about giving it to me. A wise and loving God listens patiently to my demands and only allows herself a tiny eye roll before turning me down. Then someday, when I least expect it, God graces me with good beyond anything I could ever envision. I find I am where God wants me to be, in spite of myself. This never, ever happens the way I think it should. I guess God likes to tell it slant, too.

When God breaks into our lives in unexpected, sometimes unseen, and maybe even subversive ways, it disrupts our ordinary routine. It is hard to know how to react, but a response is always called for. Like Moses or Isaiah or Jeremiah, or the thousands of saints who came before us, our first response might be one of shock and disbelief. Who me? Like Moses at the burning bush, we may even reject God's gift because we know the response can be life changing. Giving up what we are used to, good or bad sometimes, in order to follow God is scary. Yet, Jesus tells us to throw off the burdens of our present reality to find rest and joy in his arms. Writer Anne Lamott says our morning prayers should be, "Help, help, help," while our evening prayers are, "thank you, thank you, thank you."

God's love is so scandalously vast that God sent a part of God's self, his only son, Christ Jesus, to be with us and for us, even in our ridiculously messy lives, and it is through Christ we receive God's promise of hope. God's grace gives us an unexpected treasure beyond anything we might image, and our only response can be to live for Him.

Amen.

Telling Stories
James 5:13-20

¹³ Are any among you suffering? They should pray. Are any cheerful? They should sing songs of praise. ¹⁴ Are any among you sick? They should call for the elders of the church and have them pray over them, anointing them with oil in the name of the Lord. ¹⁵ The prayer of faith will save the sick, and the Lord will raise them up; and anyone who has committed sins will be forgiven. ¹⁶ Therefore confess your sins to one another, and pray for one another, so that you may be healed. The prayer of the righteous is powerful and effective. ¹⁷ Elijah was a human being like us, and he prayed fervently that it might not rain, and for three years and six months it did not rain on the earth. ¹⁸ Then he prayed again, and the heaven gave rain and the earth yielded its harvest.

¹⁹ My brothers and sisters, if anyone among you wanders from the truth and is brought back by another, ²⁰ you should know that whoever brings back a sinner from wandering will save the sinner's soul from death and will cover a multitude of sins.

One very long, very hot summer I served as a chaplain intern for a large suburban hospital. This service was part of my Clinical Pastoral Education – CPE – and it is required of all Presbyterian seminary graduates. Half the day is spent in training, and the other half in visiting hospital patients. Most of the time I enjoyed visiting patients. I was there for a friendly visit, to break up the day a bit for them, and it really didn't matter who practiced what religion, or if they expressed any faith tradition at all. If someone did want to talk about faith, and most did, I would also offer to read scripture or pray with them.

It was a humbling and exhausting experience and I complained constantly to Susan, my sainted supervisor about feeling fundamentally ineffectual. "I leave someone's room," I told her, "and think, *well, that didn't help a bit.* What did I really *do* for them?"

Susan would nod and say soothingly, "You are a listening presence." Oh. Great. A listening presence - what does that even mean? How was that making things better?

One day I visited a man who was very ill with cancer. He was pretty sleepy and medicated, but his wife wanted to talk. She was probably in her late 50s, had a distinct Polish accent, and was deeply, *deeply* angry. Her husband had been a police officer, a big, strong man who took care of everyone. He was a great family man and always looked after her. Now, he was confined to a hospital bed, helpless and racked with pain, facing a future that was far from promising. She was furious.

Like most good people who have bad things happen to them, this woman felt God was punishing them, or at the very least, not paying attention. Her husband was a good man, a man of God, a man who played by the rules and held up his end of the bargain, only to find God was not holding up God's end of things.

I mostly sat and listened while her pain and anger filled that little hospital room like a toxic cloud. More than anything else, this woman needed to tell her story. "God is supposed to love us!" she cried, "How can God do this to one of his children?"

She did not need me to offer theological answers. Instead, I listened. I said, "God is holding you close in this. God cries with you."

Well, things wound down, and I was halfway out the door when the woman called to me. I turned around and she gave me a look that seemed to burn right through me. "Who ARE you?" she demanded. I was startled, to say the least. I stammered something about being a chaplain intern, but the woman interrupted me. "NO!" she all but shouted, "you are an angel of GOD!"

But all I did was listen. All I did was pray.

James says, "Are any among you suffering? They should pray. Are any cheerful? They should sing songs of praise." In the original Greek language, the definition of one who is doing badly – *kakos* - refers to a wide range of suffering - grief, depression, ill health, bad family situations, or financial problems - anything that contributes to a negative life experience. I am sure we all have experienced situations that are *kakos*.

Our Bible translates the Greek word *thymos* as, "cheerful," but it really speaks more about the inner self or passion. An inner self that is doing well has to do more with feeling as though we are a whole person, rather than to just being cheerful.

"Are any among you sick?" James asks, then advises, "They should call for the elders of the church and have them pray over them, anointing them with oil in the name of the Lord."

When I was a chaplain, my whining to Susan about not really helping anyone stemmed from a human need to do something concrete in the face of suffering. I could not have named it then, but maybe if I had read this passage from James, I would have understood. James offers a plan of action. Not only that, there is something about this plan that elevates what can seem to us as the least we can do in a bad situation, to an action of God's kingdom. It is not "the least," it is not just the "best we can do." It is *the best thing to do*.

In fact, James offers a very serviceable way of being a community of believers. If church members actively and faithfully do as he instructs it would be difficult *not* to become a church family. James says, pray for one another, sing songs of praise, call for the elders, anoint with oil, confess to one another, and bring the wanderers back home.

As so often happens, James is writing to a very specific worshiping community about some very specific issues. We see this all the time in the New Testament. Apparently, the early church had human problems and needs right from the beginning. So this is what to do, James writes; if you are sick or suffering, you need to tell someone about it. Tell the elders of your church so they know to pray for you and visit you. It sometimes surprises me how difficult it can be for some people to admit they are sick, or in need. I cannot begin to tell you how many times someone said to me, "Oh, don't worry about me. Other people at church need you more. Don't put my name on the prayer list, other people have it worse than I do." To which I usually reply, "There are plenty of prayers to go around. If we run out, we'll make more."

In fact, I have never known prayer to hurt anybody. In Jesus' day, illness and disability had a spiritual component. If you were born lame or blind, it meant you had sinned – you were spiritually sick as well. Remember the story of Jesus healing a man blind from birth and the disciples trying to pin him down with the question: "Who sinned that this man is blind; the man or his parents?"

This is a prescientific understanding of why bad things happen to good people. Post-modern people do not subscribe to that understanding of illness and disease, or do we? We know about viruses, and microbes, and genetic influences, yet we look askance at people suffering from HIV, or opioid addition. Illness can bring undeserved shame.

Illness is also isolating. If you do not believe me, ask a chronically ill person how many friends have seemed to disappear. Fortunately, they can probably name more friends who show up at their door with a meal or for a chat. In sickness as well as sin, we are in a heightened state of vulnerability. Illness changes us. Pain changes our *thymos* – our inner selves, and our outlook on life. Our spirits suffer as well as our bodies. The term "heart-sick" has remained in our vocabulary for a reason.

Strange as it sounds, the ill and weak or sinful have a responsibility to call out to the church community and ask for help. You may not have thought of it this way, but people who modestly say, "don't worry about me" can short circuit the congregation's need to serve one another. I am certainly not blaming the victim, or saying this is easy. It is hard to reach out when you are ill and three times as hard when you have sinned. It is also not pleasant to have a visit when you are too weak to comb your hair or brush your teeth. Who wants to be that vulnerable? Yet, when our church family prays for one another it is as if the very promise and power of the resurrection remain not just some future hope but a reality that can sustain a living and active community of faith. A church that is willing to be vulnerable with each other, to confess our mutual brokenness, and is willing to step in and care for one another without judgement or lecturing, is a place where God has plenty of room to work.

There are other ways of losing a fellow church member, of course. Sometimes it is necessary to reach out in other ways. This might be as simple as inviting someone you have not seen in church for a long time to a potluck supper, or out for a cup of coffee. Even just picking up the phone and saying, "I miss seeing you," or "I have been thinking of you," can be enough. Other times it can be as challenging as sitting and listening to their pain and anger. Who knows? Perhaps they will call you an angel of God.

As I experienced in that hospital room long ago, being a listening presence, not an advice-giver or a judge makes all the difference. It is the difference between being one of Job's "friends" who tactlessly offer advice that is suspiciously like condemnation, and James, who says, "Righteous love covers a multitude of sins." We all need someone to listen to our story.

For years our church has told and heard many stories. Story after story, about good times and bad. All the while, someone was here to keep the lights on, no matter what. There was never a time when the good people of our church said, "God isn't calling us here anymore." In every decade, our church felt God's call to sing and pray, to confess to one another, visit the sick, and be brothers and sisters in Christ Jesus. God may have lit the spark long ago, but every generation of this church has carefully nurtured the resulting flame.

Amen.

The First Step
Mark 10:17-31

As he was setting out on a journey, a man ran up and knelt before him, and asked him, "Good Teacher, what must I do to inherit eternal life?" ¹⁸Jesus said to him, "Why do you call me good? No one is good but God alone. ¹⁹You know the commandments: 'You shall not murder; You shall not commit adultery; You shall not steal; You shall not bear false witness; You shall not defraud; Honor your father and mother.'" ²⁰He said to him, "Teacher, I have kept all these since my youth." ²¹Jesus, looking at him, loved him and said, "You lack one thing; go, sell what you own, and give the money to the poor, and you will have treasure in heaven; then come, follow me." ²²When he heard this, he was shocked and went away grieving, for he had many possessions.

²³Then Jesus looked around and said to his disciples, "How hard it will be for those who have wealth to enter the kingdom of God!" ²⁴And the disciples were perplexed at these words. But Jesus said to them again, "Children, how hard it is to enter the kingdom of God! ²⁵It is easier for a camel to go through the eye of a needle than for someone who is rich to enter the kingdom of God." ²⁶They were greatly astounded and said to one another, "Then who can be saved?" ²⁷Jesus looked at them and said, "For mortals it is impossible, but not for God; for God all things are possible."

²⁸Peter began to say to him, "Look, we have left everything and followed you." ²⁹Jesus said, "Truly I tell you, there is no one who has left house or brothers or sisters or mother or father or children or fields, for my sake and for the sake of the good news, ³⁰who will not receive a hundredfold now in this age—houses, brothers and sisters, mothers and children, and fields with persecutions—and in the age to come eternal life. ³¹But many who are first will be last, and the last will be first."

Does this passage from Mark make you a bit uncomfortable? I think many people find it hard to understand. It makes me feel guilty in a way, knowing that I would never have the courage to really get rid of everything in my life and become a nomadic follower of Christ. Does this mean I am a cowardly, selfish person? This passage even makes Jesus appear rather mean, but as it turns out, that is not what Jesus had in mind at all.

We can better understand this scripture passage if we set aside what we think we know about it and the fact that we have heard it a million times.

The story begins with Jesus and the disciples setting out on Jesus' last journey to Jerusalem Along the way, Jesus will try for a third time to make his disciples understand what is going to happen when they get there. Jesus will be betrayed, killed, and after three days rise from the dead. We can imagine he has a lot on his mind when a man runs up to him and falls at his feet.

Mark describes him simply as "a man." The other gospels call the man "young" or "rich" or a "ruler," so he is often referred to as "a rich young ruler" just to cover all the bases, I guess. We know three things right away: the man is respectful of Jesus, because he kneels at Jesus' feet, he calls Jesus "good teacher" in a way that is sincere, and according to the cultural perception of Jesus' time, the fact the man is wealthy means he was a good person blessed by God.

Now, if someone stopped you on the street and asked you if a person's wealth or robust good health was a sign that person was especially righteous, I think I know what your answer would be. We know – unfortunately, mostly from experience – that bad things happen to good people all the time. We also know people obtain wealth by all sorts of means, some of which are not exactly aligned with God's kingdom practices. At the same time, most of us know those who are materially at the very bottom of the ladder might be as just virtuous as the next person.

If anything in American culture today, the excesses of those top 1% wealthiest people are cause for alarm. "Income disparity" is a term handed around like popcorn at the movies. Much of what the Pope recently said highlights the crushing needs of the disadvantaged, and the increasingly wide gap between rich and poor.

Jesus was never one to buy into his surrounding culture's attitude that wealthy means you are good and poor means you are bad. In this passage Jesus even seems to indicate our ability to follow his teachings can be hindered by wealth.

The rich young man asks Jesus to tell him what he should do to inherit eternal life. Sometimes, in our concern about Jesus' next instructions we tend to skip past what he says first. First Jesus says, "Look, you know the commandments: you shall not murder; you shall not commit adultery; you shall not steal; you shall not bear false witness; you shall honor your mother and father." Curiously, Jesus slips "You shall not defraud" in there, in addition to the Mosaic laws.

It is interesting that Jesus sums up the Law of Moses using only *some* of the Ten Commandments. The Ten Commandments can be divided pretty much in half; one half speaks to our relationship with God, and the other half are instructions for living in harmony with one another. Jesus chooses to focus on those commandments concerning our relationships with our neighbors.

The young man responds, "Oh! I do that already! I've kept God's commandments as long as I can remember." Does this mean he actually believes he is perfect, or is he right, and he really is the soul of virtue? Mark says Jesus looked at him and loved him. I guess that means we as followers of Jesus should love him too, and so take what this man says to heart.

Jesus tells him, "You lack one thing: go, sell what you own, and give the money to the poor…then come follow me."

Well, the man is crushed! Perhaps he knows he can never give up all he owns. Maybe he already plans to do as Jesus instructed, and he was hoping for a bit more. We might consider that Jesus is pointing in a different direction. After the rich young man leaves dejectedly, the disciples are standing there staring at Jesus in dismay and confusion. They still believe the wealthy are righteous, and the poor had it coming to them. Seeing their expressions, Jesus remarks, "How hard it will be for those who have wealth to enter the kingdom of God!"

We can imagine the disciples looking at one another and muttering, shuffling their feet in the dust. "Listen," Jesus says, "It's easier for a camel to go through the eye of a needle than for someone who is rich to enter the Kingdom of God." Then who *can* be saved?

"For mortals it is impossible," Jesus replies, "but for God nothing is impossible."

Peter starts to remind Jesus of something important. "Look, *we* left everything to follow you – our nets and our families, our homes and neighbors!" So, are *we* good, Jesus?

I find myself asking that question too, sometimes, "Are we good Jesus?"

Yet, Jesus was not talking about money at all. He was speaking of our absolute inability to bring about our own salvation, and our total dependence on God's grace and mercy. The young man asks, "What must *I* do to inherit eternal life? What must I *do*?"

Reformed Christians know that we will never keep the commandments perfectly, nor ever buy our way into eternal life – with either money or good works. God tells us the kingdom is our inheritance, and how would one *buy* an inheritance? By definition, an inheritance is a gift, one we receive only after someone dies. Well, Jesus did die for us, and nothing is impossible for God.

Maybe wealth – keeping it or giving it away – is not the real problem for the rich young ruler. Maybe the problem is looking at what he had accumulated in this life and telling himself he had earned every penny of it. A self-made man. He reasons that if he earned every penny by what he did, maybe there was something more he could do to ensure everlasting life. Yet Jesus tells us: your salvation is not up to you. It is not about what you do or do not do to win God's heart. Salvation is a freely given gift from God; not something we can earn with good works. As one of my seminary professors used to say, "We're all just Bozos on this bus…but God loves us anyway."

So if we are all just Bozos in this life, how can we judge who is saved and who is not? We cannot, that is God's business. If we are saved by God's grace alone, can our lives be business as usual because we know we have God's forgiveness through Jesus Christ? Of course not. God cares about our lives here and now. God wants abundant life for all creation, for us, the planet, and for our neighbors both near and far.

So maybe God does care about money in a way, because God knows in the long term that the only time money can make us happy is to use it to help others. Jesus does not tell the rich young man to get rid of his money, he tells him to give it to the poor.

Giving away money is especially uncomfortable for us if we think of it in the context of scarcity. When we worry we will not have enough, we fail to see the abundance God has already placed in our lives.

Fall in many churches means a Stewardship campaign is right around the corner, but what would happen if we made time to notice God's blessing, instead? A time to remember all God has done for our church, and to begin living into God's abundance, knowing God means for us to have a full life together. Unlike the rich young man, we have no need to grieve over our possessions, because they are not markers of God's love for us. How would you spend your money or your time this week if you truly trusted in God's abundance? Think of one blessing you have recently experienced and give thanks for it. That is only a first step, but first steps are everything.

Amen.

Ash Wednesday: Getting it Right in God's Eyes
Matthew 6:1-6, 16-21

"Beware of practicing your piety before others in order to be seen by them; for then you have no reward from your Father in heaven. ² "So whenever you give alms, do not sound a trumpet before you, as the hypocrites do in the synagogues and in the streets, so that they may be praised by others. Truly I tell you, they have received their reward. ³But when you give alms, do not let your left hand know what your right hand is doing, ⁴so that your alms may be done in secret; and your Father who sees in secret will reward you.

⁵ "And whenever you pray, do not be like the hypocrites; for they love to stand and pray in the synagogues and at the street corners, so that they may be seen by others. Truly I tell you, they have received their reward. ⁶But whenever you pray, go into your room and shut the door and pray to your Father who is in secret; and your Father who sees in secret will reward you

"And whenever you fast, do not look dismal, like the hypocrites, for they disfigure their faces so as to show others that they are fasting. Truly I tell you, they have received their reward. ¹⁷But when you fast, put oil on your head and wash your face, ¹⁸so that your fasting may be seen not by others but by your Father who is in secret; and your Father who sees in secret will reward you.

¹⁹ "Do not store up for yourselves treasures on earth, where moth and rust consume and where thieves break in and steal; ²⁰but store up for yourselves treasures in heaven, where neither moth nor rust consumes and where thieves do not break in and steal. ²¹For where your treasure is, there your heart will be also.

Sometimes I struggle with my attitude toward Ash Wednesday. It can be hard to know how I am supposed to feel during a worship service that begins the season of

Lent. Faithful Christians know that Lent, like the season of Advent, is a time of preparing our hearts to receive Christ. We are familiar with the idea of claiming our own *mortality* before a God of *immortality*. The ashes we receive at the end of the service remind us we came from dust, and to dust our mortal bodies will return. From our beginning to our end on earth, our lives are always in God's hands, and it is God who will call us home when we leave this present life. Ashes to ashes, dust to dust.

What gives me trouble is how I am supposed to feel about that. After all, none of us likes a reminder of our own mortality. Personally, I find the older I get, the more Ash Wednesday seems less a time of remorse for my sins, and more a time of mourning for the ever-shorter time I have left on earth. As people of faith, we may say – and mean it with all our hearts – "Because I am in Christ, I'm not afraid to die." But that does not mean we do not follow it up with a hearty shout to God: "But not right now, please!"

Not right now because there are still quite a few items on my bucket list. Not right now because my family needs me. Not right now because I have not completed my work. Not right now because I am not living a kingdom life and I need more time to get it right in God's eyes. So, perhaps Ash Wednesday marks the beginning of a season of living with an awareness of sin and death, but also with the possibilities that come with new life in Jesus Christ. Lent is a time of asking God just how we *do* get it right in God's eyes – if we ever can, this side of heaven.

Still, God does not intend us to spend the next 40 days walking around under a dark cloud, or experiencing this awareness as a sense of doom. Ash Wednesday, if it is nothing else, is a time of being down-to-the-bone honest with God and with ourselves. We are honest about what we have done and left undone, and we are honest about whom we are and whom we are not.

In our scripture reading, Jesus, while preaching the Sermon on the Mount, reminds his listeners of the three acts expected of them as faithful Jews: they are to give alms to the poor, pray, and fast. All the Jews within hearing distance of Jesus already know that, and we should know that too. Walking in Jesus' footsteps calls us take care of the poor and reach out to the marginalized; to pray, in the Apostle Paul's words, without ceasing, and to fast. A lot of us are troubled by that last part – fasting.

Many Christians do use fasting as a spiritual discipline. My understanding is it helps focus the mind. For many reasons, mainly physical, I do not personally fast. Others fast by giving up a favorite food for Lent (and it doesn't count if you give up broccoli!). Still other people view fasting in the same way as abstaining from a negative habit during Lent.

Matthew tells us Jesus wants to move beyond the spiritual practices he and his fellow Jews already perform. It is not so much about the practices themselves; it is more about the motive and manner in which they are carried out. Jesus wants humility and honesty.

Jesus says, "Whenever you pray do not be like the hypocrites; for they love to stand and pray in the synagogues and the street corners so that they may be seen by others." I find it interesting that the word "hypocrite" is the Greek word for actor. In other words, Jesus counsels against a lot of drama around our spiritual disciplines. Do not be all style and no substance. However you travel on your faith journey, Jesus says, be authentic. Not only authentic, but also humble; after all, what can the dust say to God? So perhaps that is what we give up for Lent, our pride and hypocrisy.

Ash Wednesday calls us to repentance and reflection, and a clear-eyed assessment of the sin in our lives.

Lent reminds us that earthly possessions are the very definition of transience and insecurity; so parting with some of our resources keeps our eyes on what really matters; and what really matters in making sure everyone has enough. Although the thought is tempting, Lent is not all about inward reflection; it is also about scooting over and making room at the table for those less fortunate.

Look, God already knows we are dust. It is God who makes miracles out of dust and ashes, after all. The most important thing we ashes can say to God is a sincere admission we are not God and we know it. God will say back to us, "Yes, you are not me, but I made you and you are mine."

Amen.

The Spiritual Life: Prayer
Psalm 27

The LORD is my light and my salvation; whom shall I fear? The LORD is the stronghold of my life; of whom shall I be afraid?

²When evildoers assail me to devour my flesh— my adversaries and foes— they shall stumble and fall.

³Though an army encamp against me, my heart shall not fear; though war rise up against me, yet I will be confident.

⁴One thing I asked of the LORD, that will I seek after: to live in the house of the LORD all the days of my life, to behold the beauty of the LORD, and to inquire in his temple.

⁵For he will hide me in his shelter in the day of trouble; he will conceal me under the cover of his tent; he will set me high on a rock.

⁶Now my head is lifted up above my enemies all around me, and I will offer in his tent sacrifices with shouts of joy; I will sing and make melody to the LORD.

⁷Hear, O LORD, when I cry aloud, be gracious to me and answer me!

⁸"Come," my heart says, "seek his face!" Your face, LORD, do I seek.

⁹Do not hide your face from me. Do not turn your servant away in anger, you who have been my help. Do not cast me off, do not forsake me, O God of my salvation!

¹⁰If my father and mother forsake me, the LORD will take me up.

¹¹Teach me your way, O LORD, and lead me on a level path because of my enemies.

¹²Do not give me up to the will of my adversaries, for false witnesses have risen against me, and they are breathing out violence.

¹³I believe that I shall see the goodness of the LORD in the land of the living.

¹⁴Wait for the LORD; be strong, and let your heart take courage; wait for the LORD!

It is not often one hears a sermon about one of the Psalms, but that is what we are focusing on this morning. Our spiritual journey takes us where God always seems to lead us: to prayer. Of the four scriptures listed in the Common Lectionary for this Sunday, Psalm 27 is the only text that actually *is* a prayer; one many scholars attribute to King David.

Psalm 27 is a favorite for me and I imagine for many of you, as well. The language is beautiful for one thing. No wonder Psalm 27 is often set to music. It captures two aspects of our relationship with God: "God is our very present help, so we will not fear" and the reverse: "During life's dark times why does God sometimes seem hidden from us?" Some Biblical scholars suggest Psalm 27 was originally written as two psalms: one of praise and one asking for help in the darkness. "The Lord is my light and my salvation; whom should I fear?" and "[God] do not give me up to the will of my adversaries, for false witnesses have risen against me!"

That is the balancing act of life, isn't it? We praise, we weep, we praise again. It is the fabric of our human existence. Today, with all the violence and violent rhetoric in the world, it seems Christians must make a daily decision to trust in God and God's promises - or live in the shadow of fear.

We might say the Reformer Martin Luther was the poster boy for fear. The story goes that Luther was so frightened when caught outside during a violent storm that he promised God that if God saved him he would become a priest. Well, God did save him, and Luther kept his promise.

This did not stop Luther from being afraid, though. Most especially, he was afraid of falling into sin, of not being good enough for God, and not being good enough for God's grace. Modern psychologists might say Luther suffered emotional damage at the hands of an abusive father, and this caused him to never feel fully adequate - not for his father, and certainly not for God.

Yet, amazingly, Martin Luther was a founding father of the Christian Reformation. He was convinced we live securely in God's unmerited grace, saved by grace alone. We broken, finite people cannot save ourselves by anything we do or say. No, we will never be "good enough" but God loves us anyway.

Interestingly, Martin Luther wrote that if he had a meeting with God, and God told Luther he had changed his mind and he would not save him after all, Luther would reply, "Too late! I already have your promise."

Psalm 27 tells us, "For [God] will hide me in his shelter in the day of trouble; he will conceal me under the cover of his tent; he will set me high on a rock."

Voices shouting at us all day long tell a different story. We must fear refugees. Gun violence is so random that even our safest havens are safe no more...so we must buy more guns. Where are our resting places? Where are our sanctuaries from fear? Fear like this threatens God's gifts of hospitality and trust. Psalm 27 reminds us to choose and embrace this as the confident center of our lives: God will never leave us.

My great niece Genevieve lives with her folks near Salt Lake City, Utah. Genevieve is three years-old, going on 46. Her dad, my nephew David is, among other things, a sound and light engineer. He spends a lot of time working concerts and festivals. Last summer, there was a weeklong festival in the mountains with a special family-friendly concert scheduled for Thursday. Genevieve spent all week looking forward to the Thursday concert. That morning she asked her mother, "Can Jesus go with us to the mountains?"

Well, her mother couldn't see why not, and told her it was okay by her. Genevieve crouched down until her face was about 9 inches from the floor and yelled, "Ya hear that Jesus? You can go!"

David told this story to his mom, my sister, and concluded with, "So apparently Jesus is about 8 to 10 inches tall and likes to be invited places. "Of course, my sister replied, "Don't you read the Bible? Jesus said, '*Lo*, I am with you always."

Prayer is a way of checking in with God to reassure ourselves God is always with us. Yet, sometimes, we can feel as though God stepped away from his post. What the psalmist encourages us to do is to keep praying when the way before us is dark.

Author Madeleine L'Engle reflects: "It's a good thing to have all the props pulled out from under us occasionally. It gives us some sense of what is rock under our feet, and what is sand." I remember a line from the old hymn: "On Christ, the solid rock I stand; all other ground is sinking sand. All other ground is sinking sand."

Yet, prayer is not just beseeching God in times of trouble; prayer is also praise. For many of us, it is somehow harder to make time for prayers of thanksgiving. Saying thank you to God takes a special kind of noticing many of us forget to do. When Paul admonishes us to "pray without ceasing," I think this may be what he meant: to a kind of running dialogue with God as the day rolls on.

Sometimes prayers of praise and thanks can mean a little work on our part. We have to practice. We must cultivate a habit of noticing God working in the world. We make time to stop and pray, "Oh, this moment, this moment and *this* – how beautiful! Thank you, God."

One of my clergy friends says she prays at stoplights. No, not for the light to turn green. She prays for others as long as the light stays red. Praying for others – called intercessory pray – always makes me think of the very first scene in the movie, "It's a Wonderful Life." Do you remember? We see only the heavens, but we hear prayers for George Bailey coming from every direction. My husband and I felt as if we could hear such prayers surrounding us when he was terminally ill. It was as though he was floating on a sea of voices lifting his name to God. You may believe your prayer for someone does not mean much, but it does; *it means so much*.

Some scientific studies have been done on prayer. It feels a little weird to say that. Science and prayer – together in the same sentence? Yet, scientists have done just that: they divided people who had recent surgery into three groups. Prayers were offered for the first group and they knew others were praying for them. The second group received just as many prayers as the first group, but was not informed of this. The third group received no specific prayers at all.

The scientists were not particularly surprised in the results from group one – the group that knew prayers were said for them. Those people did well in recovery. The third group – no prayers for them! – had more post-operative infections, and fared worse than the first group. What surprised the scientists were the results from the second group – those who received prayer but did not know it. They did equally as well as the prayed for, informed, first group.

Prayers of intercession, prayers of thanksgiving, or prayers for help: all our prayers require the same thing of us: complete surrender to God. No half measures, no saying to God, "Well I've got this part covered but I'm leaving the rest up to you." No, we surrender all to God, and this can be very, very hard soul work.

As modern people we are not used to giving up control – we see it as a sign of weakness. Yet as Christians, we know we are never ultimately in charge of life, ours or anyone else's. In the dark garden, Jesus pleaded with God to spare him death on the cross. Yet he concludes his prayer with, "But not what I want, only what you want."

Jesus knew surrender and obedience to God. He is our model and guide as we journey through this difficult task. When the disciples asked Jesus how they should pray, he instructed them to say, "Your kingdom come. Your will be done" - complete surrender to God, placing God's will above our own.

As difficult a spiritual practice as surrender may be, a complete offering of ourselves to God can also be tremendously life giving. So many of us have a touch of control-freak in us, not because we desire power over others, but because we have a sense of perfectionism that makes us terrified to fail. Everyone and everything depends on us and if we do not keep all the plates spinning something dreadful will happen. We are kind of *hyper*-responsible.

I struggle with this; and I am sure many of you do, as well. When I find myself spiraling into this mode, I try to remember who is God and who is not. The Ten Commandments instruct us to believe in the one true God alone. If I am feeling hyper-responsible then maybe I am trying to play God – and to put it harshly, that is idolatry. Letting go of this false sense of responsibility is not only what God wants me to do, it is a tremendous relief! Yes! I am realigned. God is God and I am not. I am God's person: I work for God, but I am never for a moment God's own self. This also frees us from judging others. Whose faith is right? Who has God forgiven? Who is saved or not saved?

During this season of Lent, try putting down your burden of self-reliance and cast your fears on the God who longs to help you. Say to yourself: "The Lord is my light and my salvation; whom shall I fear? The Lord is the stronghold of my life; of whom shall I be afraid? Wait for the Lord; be strong, and let your heart take courage; wait for the Lord!"

Amen.

The Spiritual Life: Repentance
Luke 13:1-9

At that very time there were some present who told him about the Galileans whose blood Pilate had mingled with their sacrifices. ²He asked them, "Do you think that because these Galileans suffered in this way they were worse sinners than all other Galileans? ³No, I tell you; but unless you repent, you will all perish as they did. ⁴Or those eighteen who were killed when the tower of Siloam fell on them—do you think that they were worse offenders than all the others living in Jerusalem? ⁵No, I tell you; but unless you repent, you will all perish just as they did."

⁶Then he told this parable: "A man had a fig tree planted in his vineyard; and he came looking for fruit on it and found none. ⁷So he said to the gardener, 'See here! For three years I have come looking for fruit on this fig tree, and still I find none. Cut it down! Why should it be wasting the soil?' ⁸He replied, 'Sir, let it alone for one more year, until I dig around it and put manure on it. ⁹If it bears fruit next year, well and good; but if not, you can cut it down.'"

Jesus and his disciples are journeying toward Jerusalem when they fall into step with a band of traveling pilgrims. The road ahead is long, and to pass the time the travelers do what travelers have always done: talk about the news and share the latest gossip.

"Did you hear about that church in Charleston, South Carolina?" one person asks. "Church members were holding a Bible Study when a white supremacist suddenly started shooting. He murdered nine innocent people who were praying to God. Their blood fell on the open Bibles - It was terrible!"

"Yes!" says another, "And the hurricane down south! All those people killed, not to mention the property destruction. So tragic!"

Jesus knew what the pilgrims were doing: they were playing that age-old game of "Ain't It Awful."

"Ain't it awful what happened to *those* people (who are not us)! I wonder who is at fault? It must be negligence on someone's part. What is going to be done about it? (I'm so glad it wasn't me.)"

Well in a way, we should not be too harsh with the travelers to Jerusalem for trying to lay blame. They were only expressing what was a given in ancient Israelite culture. If tragedy struck, it was an outward manifestation of God's wrath. Someone was brought down by God's righteous anger precisely because that person – or one of their ancestors - had sinned. There was no such thing as innocent anguish. Someone was to blame.

Things are not a lot different for us today, are they? Americans in particular seem to have a difficult time with the concept, "stuff happens." People in other parts of the world don't appear to find it so hard to understand. Perhaps it is because one of our cherished American ideals is winning and always coming out on top. Hard times are something to be defeated. Death is not an inevitable fact of life, but rather something to be fought against. Life can be fixed, or someone – somewhere – is not doing his or her job.

Jesus has some sharp words for the pilgrims. Finger pointing and a system of rating *good* or *bad* in other people are quite beside the point. "So when Pilate slaughtered the worshipers, or the tower at Siloam fell," Jesus asks, "Do you honestly believe the victims were more sinful than anyone else; more sinful than each of you?"

Jesus points out that God calls us to be less concerned with the shortcomings of others and more concerned with our own character and godliness.

Still, common sense whispers to us that if there *is* such a thing as cause and effect, there must be an explainable cause to misery. One of the most heart-wrenching things a pastor routinely hears is, "Why is God doing this to me?"

Hearing such expressions of grief is a difficult but quite necessary learning for those doing pastoral care, and it happened for me during my chaplaincy internship in a hospital. Seminary fills students up with theological statements and eschatological answers, and then shoves them into a room full of tragedy and slams the door.

"Why is God doing this to me?" I heard this many times, along with its sad cousin "What did I do to deserve this?"

It must have been difficult for Jesus to resist an opportunity to defend God against charges of mismanaging the universe. He does not even remind the listeners, as Job reminded his unhelpful friends, that mere mortals cannot comprehend the mind of God. At least, Jesus does not say this overtly, but the idea of God's sovereignty runs all through this passage from Luke.

Nor does Jesus exploit human tragedy to whip up fear. Where is Jesus' claim that bad things only happen to people not aligned with our ideas of right living? Why does he not call on divine retribution for those whose family groups are different from ours or worship God in ways we find strange? Jesus does not equate suffering with God's punishment. He does not say that sin invites atrocities. Bad things just come.

What Jesus does want us to remember is that life is fragile, and that is where repentance comes in. Each day that we wake up in our right minds with a fair degree of physical functioning is a gift from God. If all of us were apportioned the good things in life based on moral consequences, no one would make it out the front door in the morning. Jesus wants to place front and center the fact that because life is so fragile and finite, we should all have a sense of urgency about repentance. It is time to drop the notion we can protect ourselves with rationalizations and false assurance.

How many of us have experienced tragedy and hardship only to find it nudges us toward God? On the other side of a harrowing episode, it is understandable to look back and see God working in our lives; to remember the fear-fueled promises we made to the Almighty; to consider why God brought us thus far and what we must do in gratitude. The more difficult experiences we have, the closer we want to inch toward God.

Jesus says, "Look, tragedy hits us so suddenly it often marks the end, not the beginning of living our lives in God. Maybe it's time to stop navel-gazing and start atoning for your moral failures." As Christians, we understand the season of Lent as a time of introspection and repentance. During the days leading up to Easter, we remember our profound limitations, and we offer the broken places in our hearts, and in the world, up to God in hope of forgiveness.

Rather than merely reacting to the dark places and events in our lives, Lent, in many ways, is a time of *forward* thinking. This a time of humbleness before God and an opportunity to live the life we get to live. Lent is a chance to look at ourselves and believe we have work to do *right now* – no deathbed confessions for us.

There is much temptation to keep Lent as a totally inward-looking season when we pray with crossed fingers that we are "not that bad and God is not that mad." But Lent is also a time to look around at who and what we have wronged, repent, and ask for forgiveness; and to – as much as it's in our power to do so – set things right. We don't often think of it this way, but the Christian outlook on repentance can be a movement toward wholeness and joy. We find abundant grace right in the middle of terrifying precariousness and the strange beauty of our fleeting time on earth.

Jesus tries to light a small fire under his fellow travelers. Repent now! Do not wait until it is too late! Make amends with God and others while you still have a chance. Then Jesus offers a little parable:

"A man had a fig tree planted in his vineyard; and he came looking for fruit on it and found none. 7So he said to the gardener, 'See here! For three years I have come looking for fruit on this fig tree, and still I find none. Cut it down! Why should it be wasting the soil?' The gardener replied, 'Sir, let it alone for one more year, until I dig around it and put manure on it. If it bears fruit next year, well and good; but if not, you can cut it down.'"

Three years should be long enough for the fig tree to become productive. By any gardener's standards, the tree has been given every chance. One of my gardener friends taught me this saying about new plants: "the first year it sleeps, the second year it creeps, and the third year it leaps." Well, the fig tree has just been sitting there looking sad, not doing any leaping or even creeping, but rather taking nutrients out of the soil which could be better used by productive trees. No wonder the owner orders it cut down.

Yet, the fig tree has an advocate. The servant-gardener asks the owner to "leave it alone" for one more year. The Greek word used in Luke's gospel is *aphes*, the root word of the Greek for "forgiveness." It's the same word used in the Lord's Prayer: "forgive us our debts." The gardener is actually asking the tree's owner to "forgive" not just "leave it alone."

Now, we run into problems if we think the fig tree can just spontaneously, as a matter of will, begin to produce fruit on its own. Rather, it has shown it is quite *incapable* of fixing itself. Only the abundant and grace-filled mercy of the gardener spares it from the ax. The gardener sees something in the fig tree and allows for the possibility it will go on to become productive.

Still, this possibility is not without cost. It requires generous and careful attention from the gardener. A little humbleness in the form of manure must be worked in at the roots. The tree must have air and light, and be watered generously. The gardener is willing to do all these things without knowing if it will have a good outcome or not.

Because of our limited, finite human lives, we know there is precious little time to get it right before God. As Michael Curry puts it, "Facing the mystery and the limits of what we can know is not an excuse to stand still and look sad."

Rather, God is before us with open arms, a Father welcoming a prodigal child. God calls us into right relationship and expects us to do our part in the form of sincere and humble repentance. Only then do we have the opportunity to grow. Christ is willing to take care of us as we figure out how to respond to this kind of radical grace, because he knows we will never get there on our own. Still, there is such a thing as waiting too long. Not because God is constantly dangling us over the fires of hell, but because we are called to be the workers in God's vineyard. We are called to ask ourselves if we are like that fig tree: bearing good fruit or just taking up space.

In the name of the Father, and of the Son, and of the Holy Spirit: Amen.

The Spiritual Life: Extravagant Love
John 12:1-11 (NRSV)

Six days before the Passover Jesus came to Bethany, the home of Lazarus, whom he had raised from the dead. ²There they gave a dinner for him. Martha served, and Lazarus was one of those at the table with him. ³Mary took a pound of costly perfume made of pure nard, anointed Jesus' feet, and wiped them with her hair. The house was filled with the fragrance of the perfume. ⁴But Judas Iscariot, one of his disciples (the one who was about to betray him), said, ⁵"Why was this perfume not sold for three hundred denarii and the money given to the poor?" ⁶(He said this not because he cared about the poor, but because he was a thief; he kept the common purse and used to steal what was put into it.) ⁷Jesus said, "Leave her alone. She bought it so that she might keep it for the day of my burial. ⁸You always have the poor with you, but you do not always have me." ⁹When the great crowd of the Jews learned that he was there, they came not only because of Jesus but also to see Lazarus, whom he had raised from the dead. ¹⁰So the chief priests planned to put Lazarus to death as well, ¹¹since it was on account of him that many of the Jews were deserting and were believing in Jesus.

Author Vladimir Nabokov wrote: "Smells are surer than sights or sounds to make your heartstrings crack." Isn't that the truth?

Pleasant or ugly, scent has the ability to transport us instantly to another time or place, and to stir our emotions.

My mother always wore *Emeraude* perfume. I guess you would say it was her signature scent while I was growing up. I have such clear memories of being tucked in bed, and my mother, dressed up for a night out with Dad, leaning over for a goodnight kiss, the scent of *Emeraude* falling in waves from her fur stole.

After her death a few years ago, I was cleaning out her dresser and found some fragile jewelry wrapped in a handkerchief. When I unwrapped it, the scent of *Emeraude* filled the room as surely as if she stood beside me. Instantly, I was four years old. I could almost feel the brush of fur against my cheek.

So what must that courtyard room belonging to Mary, Martha, and Lazarus have smelled like when Mary first cracked open a full jar of Nard? John says, "The [whole] house was filled with the fragrance of the ointment." To the recently resurrected Lazarus, the smell might be reminiscent of burial spices. To Judas Iscariot the costly Nard must have smelled like money being poured out and wasted. To Jesus, well, it probably smelled like extravagant love, and perhaps, sparked thoughts of what was to come.

Another childhood memory; if you will bear with me. My parents and I were visiting our family cemetery plot. I was standing next to a burial crypt when a sudden sharp breeze blew through the vented top of the cement crypt, bringing with it an unfamiliar smell. It took me a moment, but even as a little girl I soon realized it was the sickly-sweet smell of decay.

The simultaneous scent of life and death. I can think of no better illustration for this fifth Sunday of Lent. This is the last Sunday before the green smell of Palm Sunday descends to the rot of Good Friday. It is a hinge moment between Jesus' life and death.

Before his long journey to the cross, Jesus pauses for an evening in Bethany at the home of his dear friends, Mary, Martha, and their brother Lazarus. We know all too well what inevitably happens when he leaves this house – Jesus' triumphant arrival in Jerusalem, followed by an arrest in the garden, and the final march to the Cross. Yet, at that particular moment, the only person in the room who knows what is to come is Jesus.

Or maybe not. Perhaps Judas has an inkling. After all, it is only a matter of time before that dark night when Judas will betray Jesus with a kiss.

What a strange fellow of contradictions! Judas is one of Jesus' disciples – one of the chosen twelve. He follows Jesus so faithfully that he is placed in charge of the Jesus Movement's funds. One would think Judas must have been the soul of rectitude, the careful and conservative guy who runs the finances. His shepherding of funds is studiously controlled, never testing the boundaries of good sense, never spending beyond the budget. How admirable!

To the rest of the disciples Judas must come off as a true friend to the poor: after all, he is careful with money in order to have enough for the needy. I imagine Judas carefully calculates expenses and then informs his fellow disciples of just how much they can give in charity that week.

I also imagine Judas could be a bit sniffy and critical at times. Some people are like that. In the case of Judas, constantly offering criticism to others is a pretty crafty way of deflecting attention away from what is truly happening with the money.

Judas is a thief and embezzler, a betrayer of everything Jesus teaches, and the one who hands him over for trial. John makes sure we know Judas is upset with Mary's extravagant use of Nard not because, as Judas states, the ointment could sell for the equivalent of a year's wages and the money used to help the poor, but rather because he wants to pilfer the moneybox for himself. Judas has a strategy.

Yet the difficulty with having a strategy is that God's kingdom is not based on sensible plans. The kingdom of

God is based on a power far greater and deeper than what is in the bank account or who's who in the political, cultural or financial hierarchy. God's kingdom is foundationally one of lavish, over-the-top generosity and love. It makes no *sense;* it is beyond our comprehension; and it requires a response of extravagant faith.

Mary might see the jar of Nard as a symbol of gratitude and respect for Jesus, or as a way of showing her love for him. Judas, on the other hand, sees money and status poured out on the floor.

Oil of Nard has been around for thousands of years, and is still used today in herbal medicines and essential oils. It comes from the Spikenard plant and by crushing the roots, it is distilled into an intensely aromatic, amber-colored oil. Nard was and still is, used as a perfume, incense, a sedative, and to treat minor ailments.

In Jesus' time, Nard was also used to prepare a body for burial. More than likely, it was one of the spices the women carried with them as they walked to the empty tomb. Jesus admonishes Judas to leave Mary alone as she pours the oil on his feet, adding that she is preparing for his burial.

As John records it, Mary is utterly silent in this story. She never states the true meaning behind her lavish act. It could be argued that Mary and her sister and brother, Martha and Lazarus, are among Jesus' most beloved friends. He has eaten at their table many times, including the time he encourages Martha to slow down and Mary to keep listening.

Of course, we know Jesus raised Lazarus from the dead. He waited in emotional agony until poor Lazarus was well and truly dead, and Mary and Martha are overcome with grief and anger at his delay. So, is this dinner a way of saying "thank you" to Jesus for raising their brother?

Martha gets only two words in this story: "Martha served." Yet, Mary's actions speak louder than words. Her acts foreshadow the coming chapters of John's gospel, both the story of Jesus washing his disciples' feet and, of course, Jesus' crucifixion and death. Does Mary somehow know this is her only chance to say a final good-bye to Jesus? Along with the other women, Mary will never need to prepare the body of her risen Lord.

Some scholars have suggested that Mary anoints Jesus as king. That sort of anointing was usually done on the person's head, rather than his feet. As it is, no one ever gets to anoint Jesus' head, either, and the only time he is called King of the Jews is when those words are hammered above a cross.

Mary's second action gives us something to think about as well. She wipes the oil from Jesus' feet with her own hair. There are layers of meaning here that would have been much more apparent to hearers of John's time than ours. Most women of Jesus' day, Jews and Greeks alike, wore their hair bound closely to their heads. Taking her hair down and shaking it loose was a rather scandalous action for Mary to take. It is an intimate act. Not only does Mary loosen her hair before all the men in the room, she also touches one of them as she pours oil on Jesus' feet. Men in those days did not allow women to touch them.

People of the ancient Near East usually ate in a reclined position, so Jesus' feet would have been raised, and Mary would have bent over them to apply the ointment and wipe with her hair. If you think about it, what Mary did for Jesus could be considered intimate and even sensual in just about any culture – even ours. Is that why Judas is disgusted, or is he too fixated on the money?

Whether it is because Mary spends a year's wages on perfume, or because she openly displays a kind of intimacy with Jesus, Mary's gift exceeds extravagance – it almost exceeds good taste. Yet Jesus never objects. On the contrary, he answers Judas' remarks by defending Mary, and with that enigmatic phrase, "The poor you always have with you, but you do not always have me."

It is as if Jesus is telling Judas, "Look, I've spent my entire ministry showing you how to love the poor, but it's time for you to step up and think beyond your own needs to what's going to happen when I'm gone. Watch Mary carefully, she's showing you how to love with abandon."

I am sure this is way outside Judas' comfort zone. It might be outside of our comfort zone as well. Jesus' words, as only Jesus can truly know, fall on deaf ears. As Jesus journeys to Jerusalem, Judas is approaching destruction of his own making -- both Jesus' and his own.

To love extravagantly, to give love with abandon requires us to know and believe the extent of God's costly gift in Jesus Christ. We cannot minimize the depth of God's love for us, any more than we can pretend Jesus did not give everything for our sakes.

There is one person in the room with Jesus who might just have a glimpse of what costly love is all about. John's scripture says, "Lazarus was one of those at the table with him." I am struck with the meaning of Lazarus' presence! Jesus is not the only dead man walking in the room.

What must it be like for Lazarus? I cannot even comprehend. Is he still a little stiff and sore from his funeral wrappings? Does the scent of death still linger in his nostrils

– not quite overcome by Mary's Nard? What must food taste like and laughter sound like to one who was dead and now is alive? Lazarus – silent Lazarus – embodies the simultaneous scents of life and death.

God does not call us to a carefully parsed life of faith. We cannot look at what we possess and base our generosity on what is left over. Love is never budgeted. In Jesus Christ, God's abundant grace is visible in a way the world had never before seen. Each and every one of us are beloved by God beyond any human measure. It seems impossible to take that in, and yet we must. Because the measure of our faith is how we give love back to God, and outward to others. The poor we will always have. Scheming and greed are forever. Our only response is to love extravagantly, and let the balm of healing, justice and mercy flow down like an everlasting stream.

Amen.

Who is This?
Matthew 21:1-11 (NRSV)

When they had come near Jerusalem and had reached Bethphage, at the Mount of Olives, Jesus sent two disciples, ²saying to them, "Go into the village ahead of you, and immediately you will find a donkey tied, and a colt with her; untie them and bring them to me. ³If anyone says anything to you, just say this, 'The Lord needs them.' And he will send them immediately." ⁴This took place to fulfill what had been spoken through the prophet, saying, ⁵"Tell the daughter of Zion, Look, your king is coming to you, humble, and mounted on a donkey, and on a colt, the foal of a donkey." ⁶The disciples went and did as Jesus had directed them; ⁷they brought the donkey and the colt, and put their cloaks on them, and he sat on them. ⁸A very large crowd spread their cloaks on the road, and others cut branches from the trees and spread them on the road. ⁹The crowds that went ahead of him and that followed were shouting, "Hosanna to the Son of David! Blessed is the one who comes in the name of the Lord! Hosanna in the highest heaven!" ¹⁰When he entered Jerusalem, the whole city was in turmoil, asking, "Who is this?" ¹¹The crowds were saying, "This is the prophet Jesus from Nazareth in Galilee."

Today is Palm Sunday. Actually, the church calendar lists this day as Palm Sunday/Passion Sunday. Some churches place the emphasis on Jesus' entry into Jerusalem surrounded by a cheering crowd waving palms. Other churches celebrate this day as Passion Sunday, remembering Christ's trial and suffering on his way to the cross.

The shift to Palm and Passion Sunday was a response to the decline in attendance of Holy Week services. If folks were skipping Maundy Thursday and Good Friday services, they would move from the hosannas of Palm Sunday to the hosannas of Easter and miss the crucifixion entirely. As a result, the liturgical calendar now mashes some of the liturgy of Holy Week into the Sunday before Easter, in order to give us a chance to focus on Christ's journey to the cross.

Yet, the way I see it, something is missing without a Palm Sunday full of images of palms and joyful crowds and Jesus riding on a donkey. The problem with this approach is that after a while ministers and worship committees run out of ideas to create a meaningful Palm Sunday service. Church members know the story a little too well, and it is a struggle to find something new.

A few years ago, Doug Brouwer, the minister of my home church in Wheaton, Illinois, got creative and decided it would be really neat if an actual, live donkey came down the church's center aisle at the beginning of the Palm Sunday worship service. He thought the kids would be especially excited and would always remember this particular Palm Sunday.

Doug searched around and found a guy with a donkey. Apparently, Doug was not the only one who wanted a guy with a donkey, and the man kept pretty busy during Christmas and Easter. However, this man was available and willing to dress in Biblical costume, and walk the donkey from the entryway at the back of the church down the aisle to the chancel steps, make a right, and exit through a side door.

Well, everything went beautifully at the first worship service. The donkey was hidden until the service began. Then its owner managed to get it up the front steps of the church and into the narthex. It went obligingly down the center of the church to the delight of both children and adults.

However, the donkey apparently thought one trip down the aisle sufficiently discharged his donkey duties for the day. When the second service started, he stopped in the narthex and produced the donkey equivalent of "NO WAY."

His owner pulled and tugged on the donkey's lead. He offered a tasty carrot. He tried giving the beast a little slap on the rear to get him started. Someone from the congregation even pushed the donkey forward as the man pulled on the rope, but...well, have you ever heard the expression, "stubborn as a mule?"

Finally, the donkey made his feelings known by placing an offering on the floor of the narthex, and with that Doug gave up and his owner led the donkey away.

I like Palm Sundays with palms and parades and goofy donkeys. Yet even as a child I was aware of a certain mixture of feelings on Palm Sunday: partly joy – a respite from the gloom of Lent, but also a sort of creeping sadness in the knowledge of what Jesus would face in the coming week. I would imagine the faces of the crowd in Jerusalem cheering Jesus on, only to become an angry mob in the next minute.

In today's world, politics seem to fill the air like smoke, and I am very tired of listening to the often-nasty exchanges. Still, we cannot forget that Jesus was very political.

Jesus' triumphal entry into Israel's most important city was not a first-century version of the Rose Parade. It was a meant as a political statement to the leaders of the surrounding culture. Jesus rode into town as a returning king, and the crowds greeted him as such. The hosannas the people cried have both religious and political overtones. They greet him as God's Messiah and expect him to overthrow the Romans. Of course, the Romans take note.

Jesus was not crucified by accident, and he was not crucified just because he offended the religious authorities of the day. It was because he proclaimed another kingdom – the kingdom of God – and called people to give their allegiance to this kingdom first. He was, in other words, a threat.

For that matter, he still is. He threatens our need to define ourselves by who and what we are *against*. He threatens the way in which we seek to establish our future by hording wealth and power rather than preserving the earth for future generations. He threatens our habit of drawing lines and making rules about who is acceptable and who is not. He threatens all of these things and more. Jesus shows us the stark contrast between his humble march and the angry marches of today.

Matthew's gospel mainly focuses on presenting Jesus as the Christ, the Holy One of God, and places this image within the current culture. Matthew's culture was one of Roman occupation and Jewish authorities, both troubled by the announcement that the embodied Christ was present among them. "Who is this?" the Jerusalem crowd asks.

Matthew never suggests that Jesus comes to set up a kingdom just like that of Rome. Jesus has no interest in creating a church where people could safely worship without upsetting Roman rule or ticking off the Temple authorities.

Jesus is doing a new thing. He comes to declare a new age in human history that flips the old order on its head. In God's kingdom, the "one percent" no longer sets the rules or limits access to justice. Jesus enters Jerusalem riding on a donkey, followed by those who refute the idea might makes right; people on the margins who know a cycle of power and influence always leads to violence and death.

There is no hope in might that exploits for gain, no possibility of redemption, and evil will not be defeated through violence. Martin Luther King once said, "Darkness cannot drive out darkness; only light can do that. Hate cannot drive out hate; only love can do that."

Jesus' death comes because of his loyalty to the deepest truth he knew, and he expressed it in both his message and behavior. Jesus is found where there is suffering and despair, and every day he still comes riding into our broken lives.

Jesus' story comes to a climax this week so that the people of God can reject the current empire and begin fresh and new with the hope and promise of a good ending. Jesus announces a new kingdom, even while the old kingdom is still striving for absolute power.

Who is this Jesus?

This Jesus is the One we believe died not to make it possible for God to love us, but rather to demonstrate that God already does love us and that God's love is our only hope. This is Jesus is our true Lord, our only source of hope and healing, our singular conception of what God's kingdom should look like in the world today.

We always see Jesus through the eyes of our own culture. This calls us to ask ourselves what we are doing to enlarge God's kingdom *now*. How do we call for a kingdom of peace in the midst of an empire built upon selfishness and violence? How do we respond to a leader who tells us only he can save us when we claim Jesus as the only Lord of our life and our one true savior? For whom do we cry, "Hosanna?"

The translation of hosanna into English means, "Save us, we pray." What would we shout, if we were in the crowd in Jerusalem? What are we willing to work for now?

Even Jesus' modest ride into Jerusalem resulted in the empire retaliating against him and killing him. Will we look away and pretend Jesus' murder was just ancient Roman oppression; something our democracy today would never allow to happen? If that is true, are we also saying that Jesus' death is long gone, a relic of the past, with no wisdom for us today? Instead, do we allow ourselves to be startled into action, knowing we still live under an empire?

Hosanna! Blessed is he who comes in the name of the Lord! Peace is his goal and right relationship with heaven. Glory in the highest to the one who works for God's kingdom right here on earth. Where is that message being spoken today, and who has ears to hear it? When someone asks you, "Who is this Jesus" what will you say?

Amen.

What Kind of King?
Luke 23:33-43

³³When they came to the place that is called The Skull, they crucified Jesus there with the criminals, one on his right and one on his left. ³⁴Then Jesus said, "Father, forgive them; for they do not know what they are doing." And they cast lots to divide his clothing. ³⁵And the people stood by, watching; but the leaders scoffed at him, saying, "He saved others; let him save himself if he is the Messiah of God, his chosen one!" ³⁶The soldiers also mocked him, coming up and offering him sour wine, ³⁷and saying, "If you are the King of the Jews, save yourself!" ³⁸There was also an inscription over him, "This is the King of the Jews." ³⁹One of the criminals who were hanged there kept deriding him and saying, "Are you not the Messiah? Save yourself and us!" ⁴⁰But the other rebuked him, saying, "Do you not fear God, since you are under the same sentence of condemnation? ⁴¹And we indeed have been condemned justly, for we are getting what we deserve for our deeds, but this man has done nothing wrong." ⁴²Then he said, "Jesus, remember me when you come into your kingdom." ⁴³He replied, "Truly I tell you, today you will be with me in Paradise."

What an odd scripture lesson for the Sunday before Thanksgiving! Hard to think about turkey and mashed potatoes when Jesus hangs from a Roman cross, isn't it? Actually, this Sunday closes out our liturgical year, and next Sunday is the first Sunday in Advent, the beginning of a new church year.

Still, no matter which lectionary year we are studying, the last Sunday before Advent is always known as "Christ the King Sunday."

Pope Pius XI instituted the "Feast of Christ the King" in 1925, in an era of rising Fascism, as a statement against uncontrolled human power. In some regards, the world has not changed much since then, has it?

In recent years, some have changed Christ the King Sunday to the more appropriate, less patriarchal title "Reign of Christ Sunday." This is because so much of the world no longer can grasp what a king is and does. Certainly, a monarchy is not a familiar form of government in our country. More importantly, using the term "king" to describe Jesus threatens to miss the whole point of the gospel, because the title "king" suggests an earthly ruler and sense of order, rather than the unimaginable breadth of God's rule on earth.

Regardless of what we call it, this Sunday always reflects our Christian belief that Jesus Christ is Lord of all, and with his death and resurrection a new era, a new reign and realm, indeed a new reality, is upon us.

Coming on the last Sunday before the beginning of Advent, the story of Christ's crucifixion reminds us of the reality of God's kingdom, and of how God chooses to usher that kingdom in, both in the future and in our current context. What kind of king dies in humiliation and agony on a Roman cross? What kind of king is born to poor peasants, members of an oppressed people who live in the backwater of nowhere? Both Christ's entrance into the world, and his leave-taking signal God's willingness to do something utterly new.

Advent is coming, time to prepare our hearts for the coming of the Christ Child, but how do we prepare our hearts for the coming of this kind of king?

According to Luke's gospel, just days before the crowds in Jerusalem enthusiastically greeted Jesus, spreading their cloaks on the road, and receiving him as the one sent from God. Now he is rejected, derided by the leaders of the people, then the soldiers, and even one of the criminals hanging next to him.

Luke tells us "The rulers scoffed at him, saying, 'He saved others; let him save himself if he is the Christ of God, his Chosen One!' The soldiers also mocked him…saying, 'If you are the King of the Jews, save yourself!' There was also an inscription over him, 'This is the King of the Jews.'"

Why indeed, does Jesus not save himself? One of the criminals crucified next to Jesus even dares Jesus to save himself, and the criminal, too. He healed and saved many during his ministry – why not now? Why this inglorious ending to Jesus' earthly ministry? If he does not raise an army and slay his enemies, does that mean Jesus is a failure?

Jesus is certainly not the king everyone expected. The crowd is so disappointed and angry with Jesus they feel compelled to kill an innocent man. What sort of leader did they expect him to be?

The people of Jerusalem are frightened, worried about the shaky ground under their lives, lives that are ruled by an occupying force. They expected Rome would meet a mighty army led by a ruler equivalent to David, the soldier king. They expected Rome to be driven out.

Human nature always seems to dictate that we seek out those things and people we believe will grant us a measure of security, and who affirm our values. As it turned out for Americans, when we are frightened or feeling particularly at risk or left behind, we may even accept someone who decidedly does *not* reflect our values but who we believe will offer us security against our enemies abroad and prosperity at home. This is as true for us now as it was 2000 years ago in Jesus's time. We believe we are threatened and we want someone who promises to make it all better.

That being the case, Jesus comes as an awful disappointment. He gives no promise of winning a war over enemies, and he certainly does not promise to make it all better. In fact, he assures his followers that the cost of discipleship is huge. Jesus comes, not in power, but instead in humbleness and vulnerability.

Jesus does not vow retribution on even those who crucify him. Instead he offers forgiveness, saying, "Father, forgive them; for they know not what they do." Despite the mocking of the criminal hanging beside him, Jesus does not come down off his cross to prove himself, but instead remains on that instrument of torture and humiliation, the better to represent all who suffer unjustly. He also does not promise a better tomorrow but instead offers to redeem us today.

Today? What does that mean? When the one criminal mocks Jesus, the other criminal rises above the obvious exhaustion and pain and rebukes his fellow thief, "Do you not fear God, since you are under the same sentence of condemnation? Both of us deserve to be here, Pal, we are just paying for what we did. But this man is innocent, he has done nothing wrong." Then turning to Jesus he asks, "Jesus, remember me when you come into your kingdom." Jesus replies, "Truly, I say to you, today you will be with me in Paradise."

Today. Jesus does not tell the man that someday, in some distant future, he will be in God's presence; he says today, you shall be with me in paradise. Not in the sweet by and by, and please just hang in there.

Many Christians are more comfortable waiting for that sweet by and by than stepping out in faith. We sit out the call of Jesus while we pine for a better future. Instead of confronting the challenges and struggles of today, we try to ignore the current regime change and conduct business as usual, declaring faith to be a private affair.

If our faith tells us allegiance to Christ brings us into an entirely new way of living, God will annoyingly expect something from us. We cannot exclaim over the glory of God's work, and then ignore the degradation of our earth. We cannot keep our faith private and turn our backs on our neighbors. We certainly cannot try to manage our possessions as if they actually belonged to us, rather than understand to whom they really belong. God's kingdom is all around us, and God calls us to live by its vision and values today and always.

Jesus forgives us from the cross – both for what we have done and for what we have left undone. This sets us free. Free to stand with those who need us, advocating for them, demanding just treatment, seeing them as God's own and not a group of strangers and foreigners.

The kingdom of God is not just a matter of life beyond the present. It is in the here and now of our lives today. Salvation is not only a promise for the world to come. It belongs to the present world in which the God of all creation brings salvation through Christ. The Lordship of Jesus turns out not to be weak, or stupid, or a bad joke. It is a testimony to the way God has chosen to do things.

If we are to honor this way of God's choosing, we must raise the standards of our present culture to match what God sees as important. Money and power, and the demeaning of others are not what God intends. God's only Son came into this world a weak and helpless infant, a refugee, and he left this world a humble, humiliated servant. Turning inward and saber rattling, mocking the other, and forsaking our place in the world as salt and light is not pleasing to God. Servant leadership, working to heal and encourage, defending the weak and advocating for justice is the path of discipleship. Our present reality calls us to ask ourselves how we got so far away from God's commandments.

The people in Luke's world faced uncertainties and doubts, and so do we. Luke's world was a place where justice was for the privileged, and so is our world. First century Christians had every reason to think the world was coming apart. Those reasons are still with us today.

Yet Jesus offers an entirely new order – one of grace and hope and love - especially the kind of love that is never afraid, and never wearies of extending and receiving second chances. Even from the cross, Jesus offered forgiveness.

Yes, reading the story of Christ's crucifixion on the Sunday before Thanksgiving can be jarring. Yet it reminds us of just what we are given, and the cost of that gift. To such amazing, unearned, overwhelming love and forgiveness our response can only be one of thanks. In Christ's life and death, we have a clear look at what leadership looks like, and what we are called to do to further the work of God's kingdom here and now. Today. In Christ's resurrection, we are given the unimaginable gift of everlasting life. To that, we cannot say "thank you" enough.

In the name of the Father, and the Son, and the Holy Spirit: amen.

Easter Sunday: Only the Beginning
John 20:1-18

Early on the first day of the week, while it was still dark, Mary Magdalene came to the tomb and saw that the stone had been removed from the tomb. ²So she ran and went to Simon Peter and the other disciple, the one whom Jesus loved, and said to them, "They have taken the Lord out of the tomb, and we do not know where they have laid him." ³Then Peter and the other disciple set out and went toward the tomb. ⁴The two were running together, but the other disciple outran Peter and reached the tomb first. ⁵He bent down to look in and saw the linen wrappings lying there, but he did not go in. ⁶Then Simon Peter came, following him, and went into the tomb. He saw the linen wrappings lying there, ⁷and the cloth that had been on Jesus' head, not lying with the linen wrappings but rolled up in a place by itself. ⁸Then the other disciple, who reached the tomb first, also went in, and he saw and believed; ⁹for as yet they did not understand the scripture, that he must rise from the dead. ¹⁰Then the disciples returned to their homes.

¹¹But Mary stood weeping outside the tomb. As she wept, she bent over to look into the tomb; ¹²and she saw two angels in white, sitting where the body of Jesus had been lying, one at the head and the other at the feet. ¹³They said to her, "Woman, why are you weeping?" She said to them, "They have taken away my Lord, and I do not know where they have laid him." ¹⁴When she had said this, she turned around and saw Jesus standing there, but she did not know that it was Jesus. ¹⁵Jesus said to her, "Woman, why are you weeping? Whom are you looking for?" Supposing him to be the gardener, she said to him, "Sir, if you have carried him away, tell me where you have laid him, and I will take him away." ¹⁶Jesus said to her, "Mary!" She turned and said to him in Hebrew, "Rabbouni!" (which means Teacher). ¹⁷Jesus said to her, "Do not hold on to me, because I have not yet ascended to the Father. But go to my brothers and say to them, 'I am ascending to my Father and your Father, to my God and your God.'" ¹⁸Mary Magdalene went and announced to the disciples, "I have seen the Lord"; and she told them that he had said these things to her.

Two friends were talking about faith. One said to the other, "You know, you really should go to church more often." The other looked a little embarrassed. He said, "I'm sure you're right, I should attend church more often, but it's so boring! They only ever sing two hymns: 'Silent Night' and 'Jesus Christ is Risen Today.'"

It was a rookie mistake, but in fact, Easter Sunday - the pinnacle of our Christian year - may not be for beginners at all. We have climbed the mountain of Lent and Holy week and reached the very peak of the Christian story. Some would say we are at the apex of world history itself.

So maybe Easter is the advanced course, the final exam for humanity. Maybe Easter should only be undertaken after completing the introductory courses on Jesus' life and ministry. We could begin with the Sermon on the Mount, be caught up in Jesus' healings, his wisdom and compassion. Then perhaps we would be prepared for the great mystery that is Christ's resurrection.

Yet most people want to attend worship on Easter, even if it is a day when we proclaim the very thing most difficult to believe. I guess Easter worship can become a family tradition, or maybe it is a comfort to hear this ancient story told once again. Perhaps people come with questions.

Theologian Karl Barth once said that what brings people to worship – not just on Easter but on any Sunday – is an unspoken question: "Is it true?"

Is it true that the very God who established the laws of nature one day broke the world open by raising Jesus from the dead? Does resurrection spell out all the answers, end all problems, and wipe out the past? Is it true?

If it is true, now what? We know Easter really is not the final exam at all. There is no conclusion, and the story does not stop. Rather, we believe God resurrected Jesus to convince us that we are only at the beginning. Resurrection does not simply answer or end problems, or put everything right. Rather, in Easter God creates something new. Our Christian faith does not remove us from the hardships, limitations, and challenges of this life, but opens for us possibilities that simply would not be available had God not intervened, first in the raising of Jesus and again by entering into our own lives.

The meaning of Easter is too powerful to be called a certainty; too wonderful to live only within the boundaries of our imagination. It calls us to grab onto the power of Jesus. This power allows us to see more possibilities in the people and situations around us than we might see otherwise.

Mary Magdalene thinks she knows what she will see at the tomb of Jesus. She had been a disciple of Jesus all along, providing some of the financial support for his movement. Mary was there at the beginning and, tragically, at the end of Jesus' earthly ministry. She watched as he died, she saw him placed in the tomb, and now she seeks what comfort she can by visiting his resting place.

In the cool, dark, pre-dawn hours, Mary goes to Jesus' tomb and discovers the heavy stone sealing the opening is gone. She does not need to look inside the tomb to guess what has happened; grave robbers. Fearful, distraught, Mary runs to tell Peter and another disciple, "They have taken the Lord out of the tomb, and we do not know where they have laid him."

"Then Peter and the other disciple set out and went toward the tomb."

Most scholars seem to settle – lightly - on the idea that John is "the other disciple" or "the disciple Jesus loved." This disciple reaches the tomb before Peter arrives, takes a quick look inside, and then stands aside to let Peter enter. Peter goes into the tomb and sees empty linen where Jesus' body used to be. Then John also enters the tomb. The gospel says, "He also went in, and he saw and believed. For as yet they did not understand the scripture, that [Jesus] must rise from the dead."

John goes into the tomb and believes…believes what? If the two disciples do not yet grasp that Jesus must rise from the dead, then what *do* they believe?

Despite the fact that Jesus told the disciples many times he will be crucified and buried and then rise from the dead, they do not seem to believe it could really happen. Peter especially rejects the idea that Jesus will ride triumphantly into Jerusalem one day and be murdered the next week. Yet Jesus does die - proving to his followers that he was horribly right all along. Peter also swears he will never, ever betray Jesus…and then does that very thing. At a rooster's crow, Peter again realizes the truth of Jesus' words.

Now, Peter stands at the tomb looking at Jesus' discarded grave clothes. If someone took Jesus' body, why take the time to unwrap it first? Peter must wonder why the *soudarian* – the cloth covering Jesus' face - was carefully folded and put to one side. This is in clear contrast to the raising of Lazarus. Lazarus stumbles from his tomb still encased in wrappings. But Jesus' resurrection is not about new life that lives only to die another day. Instead, it is new life from God, and so it abides forever.

Scripture tells us very little about what Peter believed at the tomb. We learn only, "The disciples returned to their homes." Perhaps the words, "Is it true?" haunted Peter all the way home.

Soon, Jesus will make his appearance to the disciples, and Peter will realize Jesus' resurrection *is* true. It becomes the start of a new life for Peter, and the birth of Christendom. Peter, like so many of us, needs the power of Jesus' resurrection to show us possibilities rather than failure.

At the same time, John, the disciple Jesus especially loves, believes almost from one minute to the next. Without much proof, John looks and believes Jesus has risen from the dead, and his resurrection is true. Suddenly and deeply, John makes that leap of faith.

For many people, belief comes first as a gift from God, to be sorted out later. This is a raw faith followed by the slower work of putting all the pieces together. Faith enables us to move beyond believing only what we see, to entrusting our lives to the God who raised Jesus Christ from the dead.

In her book, *Take This Bread*, Sara Miles relates how she first started her journey of faith by walking randomly into a strange church because she liked the architecture. She knew nothing of Christian doctrine, and even less about the nuances of faith. She was a non-Christian, yet her next step was to participate in the Lord's Supper, and it proved to be a profoundly compelling, intensely moving experience for her. It was only then that Miles began to study this faith that was so foreign, yet so overpowering. Like the apostle John, like so many of us, she answered the question, "Is it true?" with a joyful and terrifying leap of faith.

Christianity is a new and different way of living, one that causes us to see the possibility of new life in every death, light shining in the deepest darkness, and hope in the midst of despair. Yet, it is not an easy path.

Christ's resurrection does not wash away the harsh realities of life, but it does make it possible to experience joy in the midst of fear, as God continuously creates something new. It moves us from a life we believe *we* must manage and control, to trust in the God who continually offers us grace and peace and mercy and love and life. There will always be problems and sorrows for us, but we can encounter them with the knowledge that God is always working for good in the world, and in our lives.

Easter is not a single, an unrepeatable historical occurrence. Instead, Easter reflects the dynamic and ongoing work of Christ in the world, a world God loves so much. Remember, God is not done with us, either. It is just beginning.

Christ is risen! He is risen indeed!

Amen.

Abundant Life for All
John 10:1-10

10 "Very truly, I tell you, anyone who does not enter the sheepfold by the gate but climbs in by another way is a thief and a bandit. ²The one who enters by the gate is the shepherd of the sheep. ³The gatekeeper opens the gate for him, and the sheep hear his voice. He calls his own sheep by name and leads them out. ⁴When he has brought out all his own, he goes ahead of them, and the sheep follow him because they know his voice. ⁵They will not follow a stranger, but they will run from him because they do not know the voice of strangers." ⁶Jesus used this figure of speech with them, but they did not understand what he was saying to them. ⁷So again Jesus said to them, "Very truly, I tell you, I am the gate for the sheep. ⁸All who came before me are thieves and bandits; but the sheep did not listen to them. ⁹I am the gate. Whoever enters by me will be saved, and will come in and go out and find pasture. ¹⁰The thief comes only to steal and kill and destroy. I came that they may have life, and have it abundantly."

When my husband, Tom, and I were young parents, our kids were pretty much in either the church nursery or Sunday school every single Sunday. That is because both of us sang in the choir so we couldn't sit in the pews with our children. In the summer, when the choir was on break, we frequently volunteered in the church nursery so the nice folks who watched our kids every Sunday could spend time with their own families in worship. We thought that was only fair.

One Sunday, a toddler decided he had quite enough nursery time, thank you very much, and went in search of his parents. Out of the corner of his eye, Tom saw the kid had somehow escaped through the baby gate, and was heading down the hall. Tom had very long legs, so he just stepped over the baby gate, nabbed the little boy, and brought him back inside.

Interestingly enough, rather than view Tom as the mean guy who forced him to stay in the nursery, the toddler apparently saw him as the guy who rescued him. Maybe once down the hall he realized he had made a mistake, or maybe it was a case of Stockholm syndrome, but the little guy latched on to Tom like a drowning man. I had to watch all the other kids for the rest of the service because Tom could not set the child down without a toddler meltdown.

There are gates and there are gates. Some gates lock us in, but others keep us safe. In John's gospel, Jesus calls himself the gate of the sheepfold. Over the millennium, Christians have claimed the image of Jesus as the Good Shepherd, but in this passage, he tells the Pharisees and his disciples, "Very truly, I tell you, I am the gate for the sheep… Whoever enters by me will be saved, and will come in and go out and find pasture."

Today is Good Shepherd Sunday and as I was preparing the bulletin, I had no problem at all selecting "good shepherd" hymns for worship this morning. Strange, I could not find a single "I am the gate" hymn in our hymnbook. Yet Jesus wants us to know him as the gate to the sheepfold, as well as the good shepherd.

His listeners lived in an agrarian society and would have immediately understood the image of a flock of sheep, a shepherd and a sheepfold with a gate. However, unless we were raised on a sheep farm, most of us think of sheep herding in terms of romanticized Victorian images of Jesus cradling a cute little lamb.

In Jesus' time, a sheep pen was constructed along one side of a stone barn or house. The other three sides are made up of brush topped with sharp thorns, with a rough gate in the middle. The sharp thorns and the sharp eye of the person who is guarding the pen overnight deter wolves and thieves.

Now, I think most of us know that sheep are about as dumb as a box of rocks. They are also dirty and smelly and programmed to mindlessly follow the sheep in front of them, no matter what. Sheep become so fixated on grazing that they have been known to eat their way off a cliff!

No wonder Jesus compares us to sheep. We are often unpleasant to be around, we follow along with the crowd - even if it means we head in the wrong direction, and we tend to fixate on our wants and desires to the extent that these things become a danger to us.

Yet despite all that, Jesus, The Good Shepherd knows each of us, cares for us, and holds open the gate to abundant life. Jesus as a door or gate is every bit as life giving as that of Jesus as shepherd.

It is really too bad that some readers and hearers of this passage reach in and pull out the parts of the text that seem to say Jesus excludes some people from salvation. They place a particular spin on this passage to claim Jesus is the sole source and means of salvation. I can imagine all of us here believe Jesus is indeed the way, the truth, and the life, but when it comes to knowing the mind of God, it is good to be wary of absolute assumptions. In addition, it is counterintuitive to what the apostle John most wants us to hear: that God loves the whole world and everything in it.

Humans tend to set boundaries where Jesus puts forth invitations. Today we celebrate the Lord's Supper, and our church always makes a point of inviting anyone and everyone to partake of the body and blood of Christ. Some churches – even a few in our denomination, are adamant that only the baptized can take communion. Yet Jesus tells us he has lambs in places we never think about, and that he leads them through the gate just as he does us.

Knowing who is a sinner is really God's job, and God's alone. Actually, there is surprisingly little talk of sin in our reading for today. Jesus does not say, "I came because you're a bunch of sinners in need of forgiveness." Rather, "I came that you may have life and have it abundantly." Don't get me wrong, I believe that all of our lives and actions and very beings are tainted by sin. Yet, as I read passages like this -- or that other central passage, John 3:16, I am struck that the operative terms are not always, or even regularly, sin and forgiveness but rather life and light and love and abundance. Which leads me to wonder if we understand and talk about the salvation Jesus brings in too narrow a way.

When my friend Sue was a little girl, both of her parents worked the nightshift for a daily newspaper. Sue was an only child and knew how to play quietly during the day while her parents slept. One day when Sue was about five years old, the doorbell rang, and when she answered it, there were two serious-looking men in white shirts and dark ties standing on the porch. In a booming voice, one of the men asked, "Little girl, do you want to be saved?"

Sue looked him up and down and declared, "I don't need to be saved. I'm a PRESBYTERIAN!" and slammed the door shut.

Maybe when Jesus said, "I came that they may have life, and have it abundantly" he was saying salvation is more than forgiveness. It is also an invitation to live into abundant life.

Salvation is often understood as the erasure of our sin and failure alone, rather than the creation of new life and possibility. Forgiveness of sin is wonderful, of course, but it occurs to me that if that is all we understand salvation to be we are, at best, back to square one and miss that Jesus offers not just life, but life in its abundance.

Reading from the Common Lectionary cheats us in a way because it selects only this short piece of scripture from what is actually a long story. The story begins when Jesus heals the man born blind, and goes all the way through to the passage following our reading for today, the passage where Jesus says, "I am the good shepherd. The good shepherd lays down his life for the sheep."

So when we hear our scripture lesson for today, we must see the crowd surrounding Jesus includes not only his disciples, but also the Pharisees, and most important – the man born blind who is now healed by Jesus. Everyone is still there, right outside the temple where the blind man was given his sight, and exclaimed, "Lord, I believe!"

In John's gospel, salvation means the man born blind will now know sustenance and security, and an entirely new way of life. For the disciples, Jesus' words to the blind man are in reality for them too: for every disciple, and every believer.

At the heart of the Gospel is the resurrection promise of life and possibility and potential and power. The miracle that we are saved *from* something but also *for* something: for life in all its abundance here and now.

This invites us to imagine that abundant life – and perhaps salvation itself – is best understood in each individual's personal context. For the blind man, abundance is sight. For the single parent it might be companionship and help. For the impoverished neighborhood, it might be dignity and the chance of self-determination. Abundant life looks different in different places and to different people, but it always manifests itself as a response to whatever seeks to rob the children of God of their inheritance of life, purpose, and joy.

What part of your life is trying to rob you of the life God imagines for you? You are saved from sin and death, but what are you saved for? Maybe in this passage there is a profound invitation for us not simply to *listen to* Jesus' promise of salvation and abundant life but actually *to live into* it. How? By joining ourselves to his mission. That means, of course, that we must pay attention to what is robbing our neighbors of life, and then stand with them against those forces, so that they might have not just life, but life in abundance.

Abundant life is not simply a promise about some distant eternal future, but is a concrete invitation to discover life right now by extending it to those around us. Salvation is not the forgiveness of sin alone, but it is also a commission by Jesus to help others experience their own abundant life. Church is not just the place where we go to hear about abundant life but the place that sends us out to experience and share it with the world God loves so much.

Amen.

Seeking: Epiphany Sunday
Matthew 2:1-12

2In the time of King Herod, after Jesus was born in Bethlehem of Judea, wise men from the East came to Jerusalem, ²asking, "Where is the child who has been born king of the Jews? For we observed his star at its rising, and have come to pay him homage." ³When King Herod heard this, he was frightened, and all Jerusalem with him; ⁴and calling together all the chief priests and scribes of the people, he inquired of them where the Messiah was to be born. ⁵They told him, "In Bethlehem of Judea; for so it has been written by the prophet: ⁶'And you, Bethlehem, in the land of Judah, are by no means least among the rulers of Judah; for from you shall come a ruler who is to shepherd my people Israel.'" ⁷Then Herod secretly called for the wise men and learned from them the exact time when the star had appeared. ⁸Then he sent them to Bethlehem, saying, "Go and search diligently for the child; and when you have found him, bring me word so that I may also go and pay him homage."

⁹When they had heard the king, they set out; and there, ahead of them, went the star that they had seen at its rising, until it stopped over the place where the child was. ¹⁰When they saw that the star had stopped, they were overwhelmed with joy. ¹¹On entering the house, they saw the child with Mary his mother; and they knelt down and paid him homage. Then, opening their treasure chests, they offered him gifts of gold, frankincense, and myrrh. ¹²And having been warned in a dream not to return to Herod, they left for their own country by another road.

King Herod is frightened, and when a powerful ruler is frightened, he has ways of ensuring that all around him are frightened as well. "The time of King Herod" as Matthew calls it, is not a good, happy, or peaceful time.

Herod reigned from 37 to 4 B.C. He was an Idumean – a non-Jew – appointed by the Roman Senate to rule over Jerusalem and surrounding areas, and he was ruthless. Herod murdered his wife, three of his sons (by strangling them), his mother-in-law, brother-in-law, uncle and many others. When someone is power-driven and arrogant, life is cheap, and being close to Herod was dangerous. Part of Herod's problem is that he is not a real king. He is a puppet of the Roman Empire, and as we know, power and insecurity are not a good mix.

In addition, Herod the Great has a love of showmanship. He created splendid monuments, theaters, fortresses and amphitheaters. Perhaps his greatest work was the rebuilding of the Temple in Jerusalem, which took more than 40 years to complete.

At the beginning of Matthew's scripture passage, we meet the other characters in this story: three "Wise Men" who unknowingly collide with Herod's politics and pride. Wise Men, Magi, or Kings: these visitors from the east are shrouded in mystery for us today.

Magi (as in magicians) might have belonged to a priestly caste called Zoroastrians. This caste studied astrology, which at that time was considered a science. Tradition has it that the Magi were of noble birth, educated, wealthy and influential. Some accounts say they were philosophers, the counselors of rulers, and learned in all wisdom of the ancient East. Perhaps they were Persians, or from Yemen, although many scholars believe the Magi were from Babylon, or Syria, as we know it today.

The Wise Men came from the east, and the Greek word for east – *anatole* – means "the rising," like the rising of the sun. Isaiah tells us: "Arise, shine; for your light has come." Isaiah's vision of Israel's salvation includes a pilgrimage of all nations, drawn to the light of God. So for Matthew, and later on during the work of the apostle Paul, three wise travelers from Far Eastern cultures and ethnicities represent a moment when the gospel of Christ opens to all the nations of the world: Jew and Gentile alike.

Still, no matter who they are, the strangers from the east are seekers. They left all the comforts of home and set out on a dangerous journey; fueled by hope that a bright star would lead them to a newborn king, such as they had never seen before. Historians have tried very hard to determine if the star of Bethlehem was a celestial event like a comet, or the special alignment of stars. Maybe we do not really need to know if it was an extraordinary star, or if it was an ordinary star, created by God to be seen through the eyes of extraordinary people.

Certainly, the three seekers must have been people of good will, as well. I say that because they approach Herod's court with the kind of innocence often born of good intentions; they believe Herod is just as genuinely interested in the baby king as they are. Herod is interested, all right, just not in the same way. This is the point at which our story can remain a comfortable Christmas tale of three Wise Men bringing gifts to baby Jesus, or it can take a darker turn.

Herod calls together the chief priests and scribes - the religious establishment, the power elite, to help him figure out just where to find this dangerous little baby. Of course, Herod is up to no good.

His advisors search the scriptures looking at the words of prophets, finding signs that point to the birth of God's Chosen One. To everyone's surprise this is prophesized to be in a sleepy little backwater town to peasant parents. We can imagine that those at the center of power are stunned to find God at work where no one thinks to look.

We are not surprised when Herod reacts in fear and with vengeance. He calls the Wise Men to him, and with an oily smile, he encourages his visitors from the east to go and search diligently for the child using the directions he supplies. He even waters their camels and packs them a nice lunch. Then Herod makes a request, "when you have found the little king, bless his heart, bring me word so that I may also go and pay him homage." *How nice*, the Wise Men think, and off they go.

No matter what the three Kings actually think about Herod, one thing is certain: their devotion to finding Jesus is impressive. These travelers are not Jews so they do not have scriptures to guide them, as did Herod's advisors. They have not been told all their lives that God would send a messiah to save them. Yet they saw something that drove them to leave their own country and search for a new king, and in doing so, these strangers from the east bring tidings of great joy to people who walked in darkness.

Matthew offers us characters that could not stand in greater contrast to one another, both in Matthew's time and in ours. Some people seek Jesus but do not know where to look, while others know exactly where to look but are afraid to find Jesus for themselves. Herod is motivated by fear he will be usurped by a new king, and he decides to act.

The Wise Men do indeed find the baby Jesus in a modest home, cradled by his teen-aged mother. So great is their faith that – appearances aside – they know they have at last found the King of Kings. They are overwhelmed with joy, as Matthew tells it. They kneel down and pay Jesus homage. Finally, the three seekers open their precious packages and offer him gifts of gold, frankincense and myrrh. We take note of the order in which the Wise Men approach Jesus: offering themselves first and the material gifts second.

The Wise Men are warned in a dream not to return to Herod, so they quietly leave the holy family and go back to their own country by a different way. Although it is not in our reading for today, we know that brutal Herod responded in an unspeakable way by killing all little boys of Jesus' age. The best and the worst of human nature springs up in response to God's gift of revelation.

It is haunting to consider that the slaughter of innocents occurs again and again in our modern context in places like Aleppo or Somalia, or Myanmar. Why does a Herod have to live in every age and in so many different horrifying expressions?

God's grace is wonderful and astounding, and frightening at the same time. When we consider the Three Kings as scientists who practice a different religion and come from Middle Eastern countries, it takes on new meaning for us today. Will that knowledge cause us to expand our ideas of God's love, or do we join Herod in feeling threatened?

The Herods of our day do not listen for Christ's call or obey his commandments. How can they and still act as they do? They have forgotten the leadership Jesus commands is servant leadership as Jesus modeled it. They have forgotten God places them in their positions to serve rather than to be served.

As Christians, we are called to testify to the far-reaching implications of Jesus' birth, and witness to God's commitment to the whole world…with no exceptions. As Christians, we continually seek Jesus with an awareness that we really *do* know where to find him, if only we have the courage to look. Christ tells us to look for his face among the poor and the outcasts, the powerless and forgotten. Jesus comes to us in the Eucharist, and anywhere two or more gather in his name. We find him in scripture, and in the Spirit we receive at our baptism. We know where to look, and we know how to guide others to the Christ Child.

Perhaps that is why Matthew's scripture has a darker heart than Luke's does. We love Luke with his familiar angels and shepherds, but in Matthew, with his story of mad King Herod, we understand it is into this messy and difficult world God comes to us in the saving grace of Jesus Christ. He appears in the middle of people so burdened by fear that we often do unthinkable things to each other…and to ourselves. It is to us, the ones with the gaping, God-sized holes in our hearts that Jesus comes to be God with us, no matter what. It is to us humble, broken, stubborn people that God urgently calls to speak up for what is right.

Amen.

www.ingramcontent.com/pod-product-compliance
Lightning Source LLC
Chambersburg PA
CBHW052138110526
44591CB00012B/1779

9 781949 888386